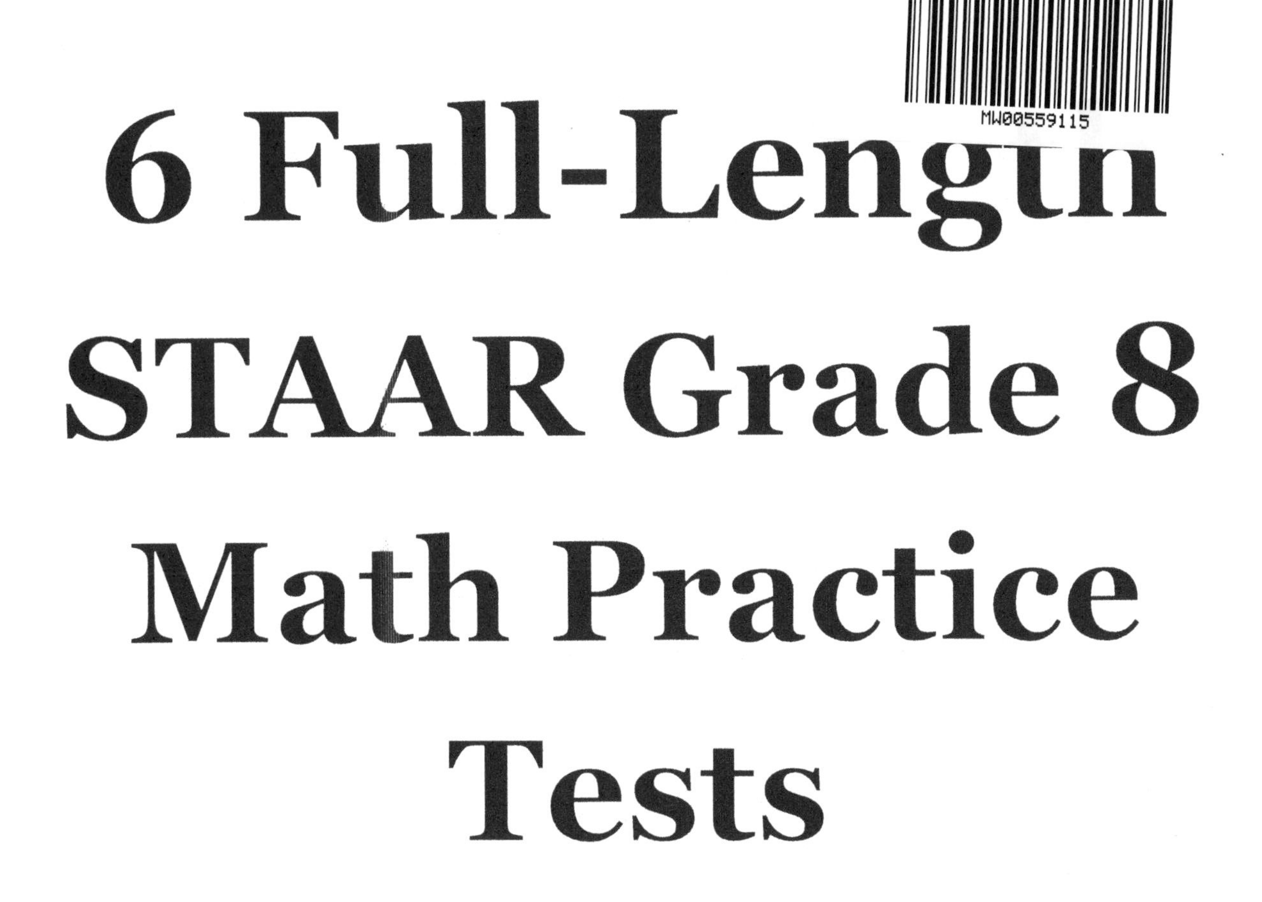

6 Full-Length STAAR Grade 8 Math Practice Tests

Extra Test Prep to Help Ace the STAAR Math Test

By

Michael Smith & Reza Nazari

6 Full-Length STAAR Grade 8 Math Practice Tests

Published in the United State of America By

The Math Notion

Web: WWW.MathNotion.Com

Email: info@Mathnotion.com

About the Author

Michael Smith has been a math instructor for over a decade now. He holds a master's degree in Management. Since 2006, Michael has devoted his time to both teaching and developing exceptional math learning materials. As a Math instructor and test prep expert, Michael has worked with thousands of students. He has used the feedback of his students to develop a unique study program that can be used by students to drastically improve their math score fast and effectively.

– SAT Math Practice Book

– ACT Math Practice Book

– GRE Math Practice Book

– Common Core Math Practice Book

–many Math Education Workbooks, Exercise Books and Study Guides

As an experienced Math teacher, Mr. Smith employs a variety of formats to help students achieve their goals: He tutors online and in person, he teaches students in large groups, and he provides training materials and textbooks through his website and through Amazon.

You can contact Michael via email at:
info@Mathnotion.com

Prepare for the STAAR Math test with a perfect practice book!

The surest way to practice your STAAR Math test-taking skills is with simulated exams. This comprehensive practice book with 6 full length and realistic STAAR Math practice tests help you measure your exam readiness, find your weak areas, and succeed on the STAAR Math test. The detailed answers and explanations for each STAAR Math question help you master every aspect of the STAAR Math.

6 Full-length STAAR Math Practice Tests is a prestigious resource to help you succeed on the STAAR Math test. This perfect practice book features:

- Content 100% aligned with the STAAR test
- Six full-length STAAR Math practice tests similar to the actual test in length, format, question types, and degree of difficulty
- Detailed answers and explanations for the STAAR Math practice questions
- Written by STAAR Math top instructors and experts

After completing this hands-on exercise book, you will gain confidence, strong foundation, and adequate practice to succeed on the STAAR Math test.

Contents

STAAR Math Practice Tests

Time to Test

Time to refine your skill with a practice examination

Take a REAL STAAR Mathematics test to simulate the test day experience.

After you've finished, score your test using the answer key.

Before You Start

- You'll need a pencil, calculator, and a timer to take the test.
- It's okay to guess. You won't lose any points if you're wrong.
- After you've finished the test, review the answer key to see where you went wrong.

Graphing calculators are permitted for STAAR Tests Grade 8

Good Luck!

STAAR GRADE 8 MAHEMATICS REFRENCE MATERIALS

Linear Equations		
Slope-intercept form		$y = mx + b$
Slope of a line		$m = \frac{y_2 - y_1}{x_2 - x_1}$
Circumference		
Circle	$C = 2\pi r$ or	$C = \pi d$
Area		
Triangle		$A = \frac{1}{2}bh$
Rectangle or Parallelogram		$A = bh$
Trapezoid		$A = \frac{1}{2}h(b_1 + b_2)$
Circle		$A = \pi r^2$
Surface Area		
	Lateral	**Total**
Prism	$S = ph$	$S = ph + 2B$
Cylinder	$S = 2\pi rh$	$S = 2\pi rh + 2\pi r^2$
Volume		
Prism or cylinder		$V = Bh$
Pyramid or Cone		$V = \frac{1}{3}Bh$
Sphere		$V = \frac{4}{3}\pi r^3$
Additional Information		
Pythagorean theorem		$a^2 + b^2 = c^2$
Simple interest		$I = prt$
Compound interest		$I = p(1 + r)^t$

State of Texas Assessments of Academic Readiness

STAAR Practice Test 1

Mathematics

GRADE 8

Administered *Month Year*

1) The area of a circle is 49 π. Which of the following can be the circumference of the circle?

A. 14 π

B. 49 π

C. 21 π

D. 10 π

2) You can buy 12 cans of green beans at a supermarket for $5.40. How much does it cost to buy 42 cans of green beans?

A. $7.78

B. $18.90

C. $15.75

D. $226.8

3) Which of the following is the solution of the following inequality?

$$7x - 5 > 17x - 8.5 - 6.5x$$

A. $x < 1$

B. $x > 1$

C. $x < -1$

D. $x > -1$

4) What is the perimeter of a square that has an area of 349.69 feet?

Write your answer in the box below.

5) A tree 12 feet tall casts a shadow 39 feet long. Jack is 5 feet tall. How long is Jack's shadow?

A. 3.25 ft

B. 16.25 ft

C. 7.80 ft

D. 93.60 ft

6) The price of a laptop is decreased by 15% to $425. What is its original price?

A. 450

B. 488.75

C. 63.75

D. 500

7) A container holds 4.5 gallons of water when it is $\frac{9}{34}$ full. How many gallons of water does the container hold when it's full?

A. 18

B. 17

C. 7.5

D. 15

8) If $(4^a)^b = 256$, then what is the value of $a \times b$?

A. $4a$

B. $4b$

C. 4

D. 8

9) A bag contains 20 balls: six green, three black, five blue, four red and two white. If 18 balls are removed from the bag at random, what is the probability that a white ball has been removed?

A. $\frac{1}{10}$

B. $\frac{9}{10}$

C. $\frac{2}{18}$

D. $\frac{9}{20}$

10) What is the x-intercept of the line with equation $-3x + 5y = -21$?

A. -3

B. $+5$

C. $+7$

D. $-\frac{5}{21}$

11) Which of the following expressions is equivalent to

$3xy(x - y)$?

A. $3yx^2 - 3xy$

B. $3x^2 - 3y^2$

C. $-3xy^2 + 3x^2y$

D. $3xy^2 - 3yx^2$

12) A soccer team played 150 games and won 34 percent of them. How many games did the team win?

A. 126

B. 99

C. 34

D. 51

13) The equation of a line is given as: $y = -2x + 1$. Which of the following points does not lie on the line?

A. $(-1, 3)$

B. $(0, 1)$

C. $(3, -5)$

D. $(1, -2)$

14) The perimeter of the trapezoid below is 36 cm. What is its area?

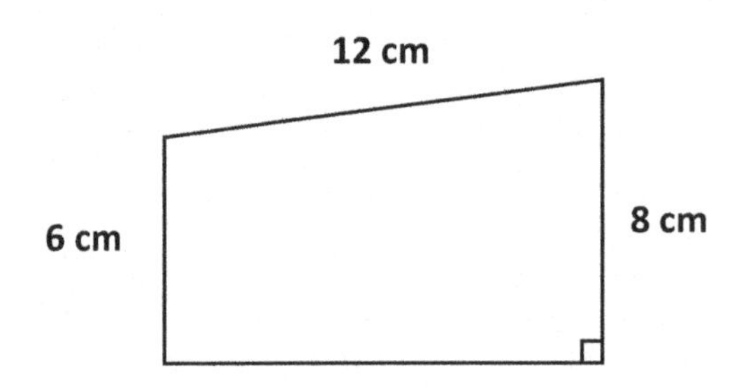

Write your answer in the box below.

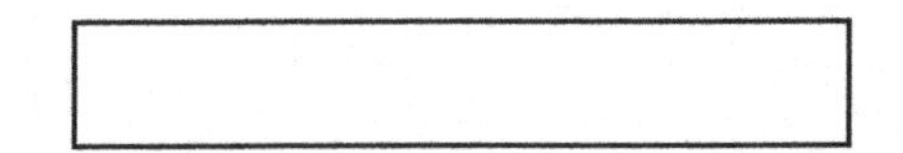

15) Which graph does not represent y as a function of x?

A.

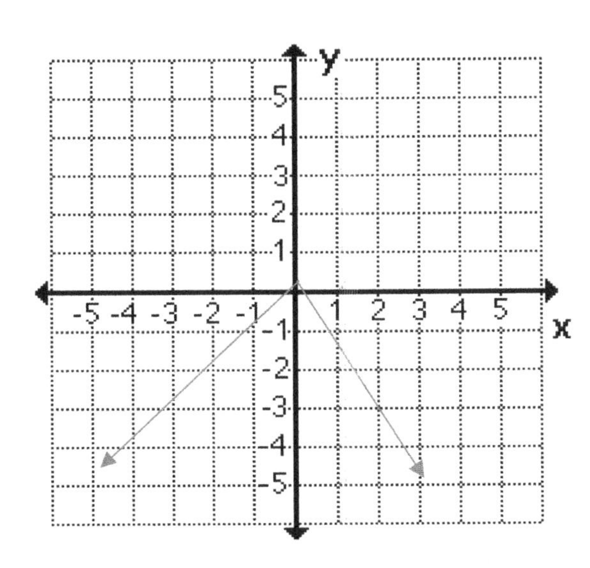

B.

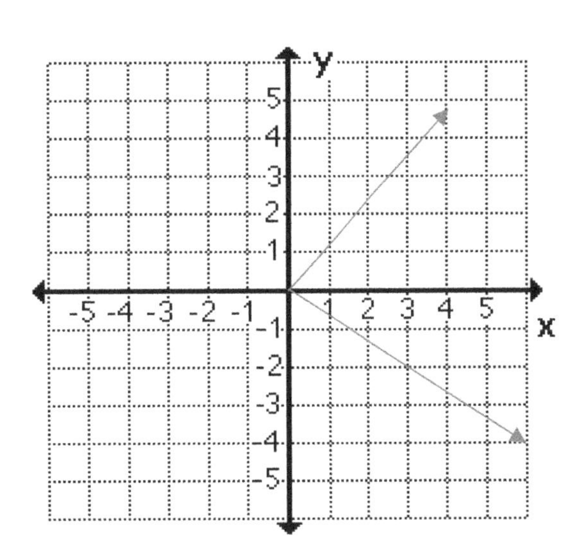

C.

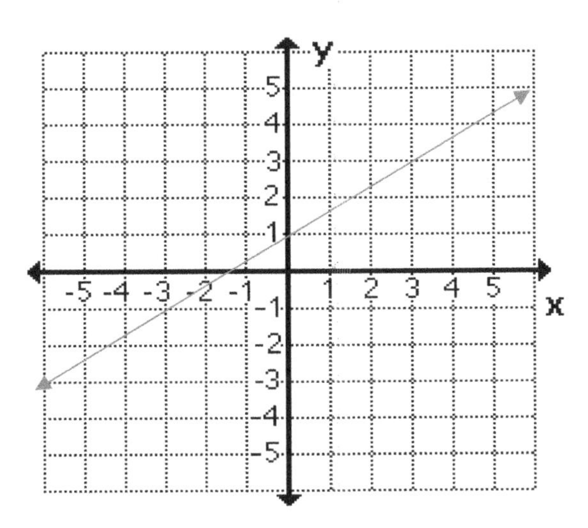

D.

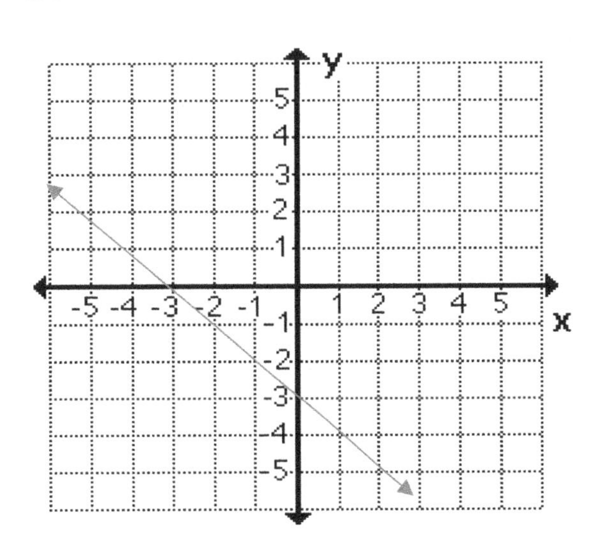

16) Which of the following is equivalent to $-23 < -5x + 2 < 2$?

A. $-5 < x < 0$

B. $0 < x < 5$

C. $5 < x < 0$

D. $-5 < x < -5$

17) A bank is offering 2.05% simple interest on a savings account. If you deposit $16,000, how much interest will you earn in five years?

A. $820

B. $1,640

C. $3,280

D. $164

18) Joe scored 22 out of 25 marks in Algebra, 42 out of 50 marks in science and 17 out of 20 marks in mathematics. In which subject his percentage of marks is best?

A. Algebra

B. Science

C. Mathematics

D. Algebra and Science

19) What is the volume of the following triangular prism?

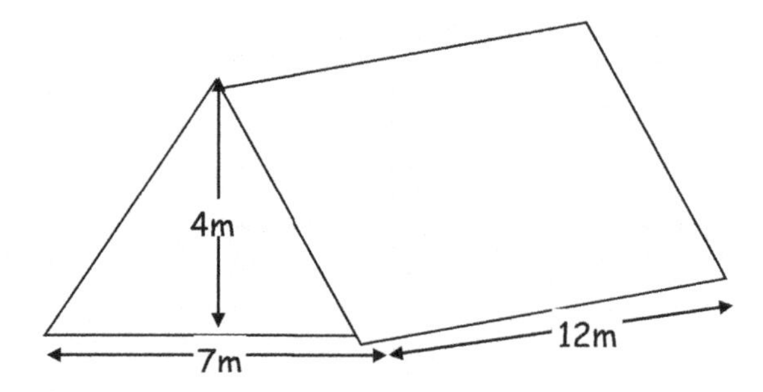

Write your answer in the box below.

20) The marked price of a computer is E Euro. Its price decreased by 15% in March and later increased by 6 % in April. What is the final price of the computer in E Euro?

A. 0.79 E

B. 0.091E

C. 0.91 E

D. 0.901 E

21) Find the slope–intercept form of the graph $2x - 6y = -15$

A. $y = 3x + \frac{2}{5}$

B. $y = \frac{1}{3}x + \frac{2}{5}$

C. $y = \frac{1}{3}x + 2\frac{1}{2}$

D. $y = \frac{1}{3}x - 2\frac{1}{2}$

22) Triangle ABC is graphed on a coordinate grid with vertices at A (4, 0), B (–2, 5) and C (3, 8). Triangle ABC is reflected over x axes to create triangle A' B' C'. Which order pair represents the coordinate of C'?

A. $(8, 3)$

B. $(-3, -8)$

C. $(3, -8)$

D. $(-3, 8)$

23) Which of the following point is the solution of the system of equations?

$$\begin{cases} 2x + 3y = -2 \\ 5x - y = 12 \end{cases}$$

A. $(-2, 2)$

B. $(2, -2)$

C. $(-1, 0)$

D. $(5, -4)$

24) A shirt costing \$300 is discounted 20%. After a month, the shirt is discounted another 10%. Which of the following expressions can be used to find the selling price of the shirt?

A. $(300)(0.20)(0.10)$

B. $(300)(0.80)(0.90)$

C. $(300)\ (0.20) - (240)\ (0.10)$

D. $(300)(0.20) - (300)(0.10)$

25) What is the distance between the points $(2, 0)$ and $(-1, 4)$?

A. 2

B. 7

C. 4

D. 5

Questions 26 and 27 are based on the following data

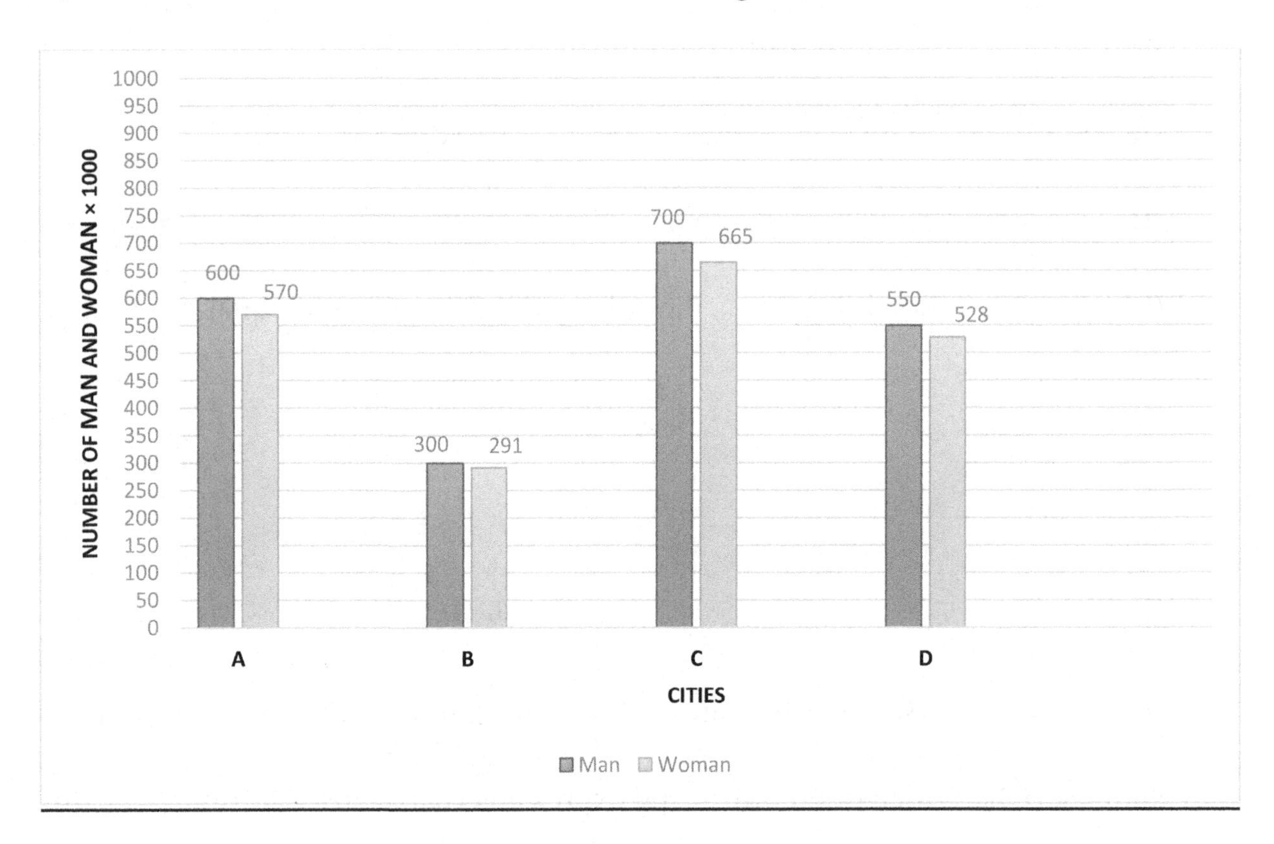

26) What's the ratio of percentage of men in city C to percentage of women in city B?

A. 0.10

B. 0.01

C. 0.99

D. 1.01

27) What's the minimum ratio of woman to man in the four cities?

A. 0.98

B. 0.97

C. 0.96

D. 0.95

28) Line m passes through the point $(3, -4)$. Which of the following **CANNOT** be the equation of line m?

A. $y = -4$

B. $y = 2x - 10$

C. $y = 1 - x$

D. $y = -x - 1$

29) The sum of three numbers is 62. If another number is added to these three numbers, the average of the four numbers is 24. What is the fourth number?

A. 24

B. 34

C. 30.50

D. 13

30) David owed $13,202. After making 39 payments of $278 each, how much did he have left to pay?

A. $2360

B. $3660

C. $1360

D. $2780

31) Which of the following lines is parallel to the graph of $y = 3x - 2$?

A. $3x - 2y = 4$

B. $2x - 3y = 0$

C. $3x - y = -4$

D. $2x + y = 4$

32) The average of four consecutive numbers is 28.5. What is the smallest number?

A. 24

B. 28

C. 27

D. 32

33) The price of a laptop is decreased by 15% to $425. What is its original price?

A. 450

B. 488.75

C. 63.75

D. 500

34) The average weight of 16 girls in a class is 37 kg and the average weight of 24 boys in the same class is 42 kg. What is the average weight of all the 50 students in that class?

A. 39 Kg

B. 39.50 Kg

C. 40 Kg

D. 40.50 Kg

35) Liam's average (arithmetic mean) on two mathematics tests is 90. What should Liam's score be on the next test to have an overall of 92 for all the tests?

A. 98

B. 85

C. 96

D. 95

36) Which of the following equations has a graph that is a straight line?

A. $y = x^2 - 4$

B. $y^2 - x^2 = 4$

C. $x - y = 4$

D. $x + xy = 4$

37) An angle is equal to one eighth of its supplement. What is the measure of that angle?

A. 60

B. 45

C. 30

D. 20

38) Three fourth of 32 is equal to $\frac{4}{5}$ of what number?

A. 30

B. 24

C. 16

D. 40

39) A card is drawn at random from a standard 52–card deck, what is the probability that the card is of Diamonds? (The deck includes 13 of each suit clubs, diamonds, hearts, and spades)

A. $\frac{4}{52}$

B. $\frac{1}{4}$

C. $\frac{1}{52}$

D. $\frac{1}{13}$

40) The score of Zoe was one third of Emma and the score of Harper was twice that of Emma. If the score of Harper was 84, what is the score of Zoe?

A. 14

B. 24

C. 42

D. 28

Practice Test 1

This is the End of this Section.

State of Texas Assessments of Academic Readiness

STAAR Practice Test 2

Mathematics

GRADE 8

Administered *Month Year*

1) Right triangle ABC has two legs of lengths 18 cm (AB) and 24 cm (AC). What is the length of the third side (BC)?

A. 30 cm
C. 16 cm
B. 24 cm
D. 18 cm

2) When a number is subtracted from 35 and the difference is divided by that number, the result is 4. What is the value of the number?

A. 12
C. 8
B. 7
D. 4

3) A bank is offering 2.25% simple interest on a savings account. If you deposit $6,000, how much interest will you earn in four years?

A. $54
C. $540
B. $135
D. $1350

4) In a party, 15 soft drinks are required for every 9 guests. If there are 117 guests, how many soft drinks is required?

A. 13
C. 195
B. 135
D. 225

5) A chemical solution contains 6% alcohol. If there is 14.4 ml of alcohol, what is the volume of the solution?

A. 420 ml
C. 360 ml
B. 240 ml
D. 480 ml

6) What is the area of the shaded region?

A. 105

B. 36

C. 18

D. 69

7 ft

9 ft

4 ft

15 ft

7) A rope weighs 450 grams per meter of length. What is the weight in kilograms of 13.4 meters of this rope? (1 kilograms = 1000 grams)

A. 0.63

B. 0.6030

C. 6.03

D. 60.30

8) The ratio of boys to girls in a school is 3:4. If there are 490 students in a school, how many boys are in the school.

Write your answer in the box below.

9) In two successive years, the population of a town is increased by 8% and 15%. What percent of the population is increased after two years?

A. 16.2%

B. 24.2%

C. 120%

D. 20 %

10) Which graph shows a non–proportional linear relationship between x and y?

A.

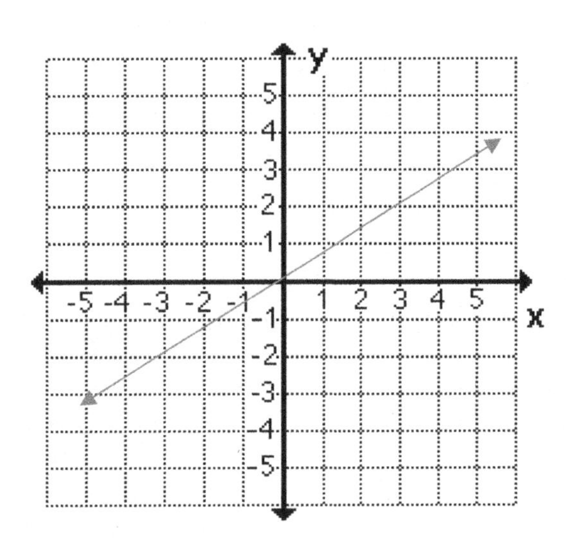

B.

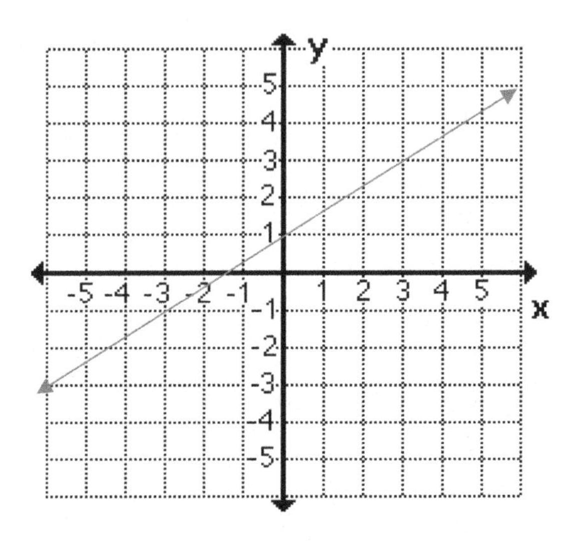

C.

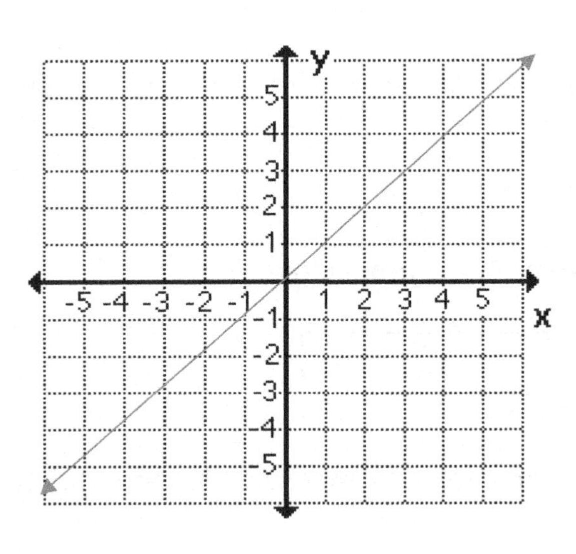

D.

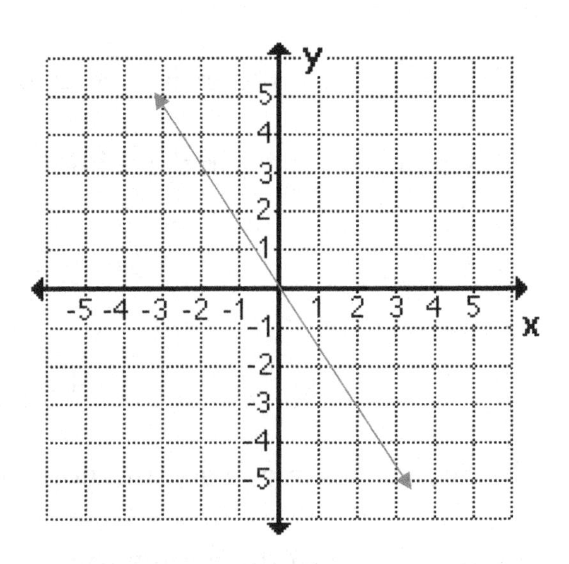

11) four years ago, Amy was four times as old as Mike was. If Mike is 9 years old now, how old is Amy?

A. 24

B. 20

C. 16

D. 13

12) What is the value of $|-21+7|-|7(-3)|$?

A. -7

B. $+7$

C. -35

D. $+49$

13) What is the solution of the following system of equations?

$$\begin{cases} \dfrac{-x}{3}+\dfrac{y}{6}=2 \\ \dfrac{-2y}{5}+2x=-6 \end{cases}$$

A. $x=-3, y=6$

B. $x=12, y=36$

C. $x=9, y=30$

D. $x=-1, y=10$

14) If a gas tank can hold 28 gallons, how many gallons does it contain when it is $\frac{5}{7}$ full?

A. 39.2

B. 26

C. 21

D. 20

15) What is the length of BC in the following figure if AB = 6, DF = 8 and BD = 35?

A. 15

B. 14

C. 20

D. 24

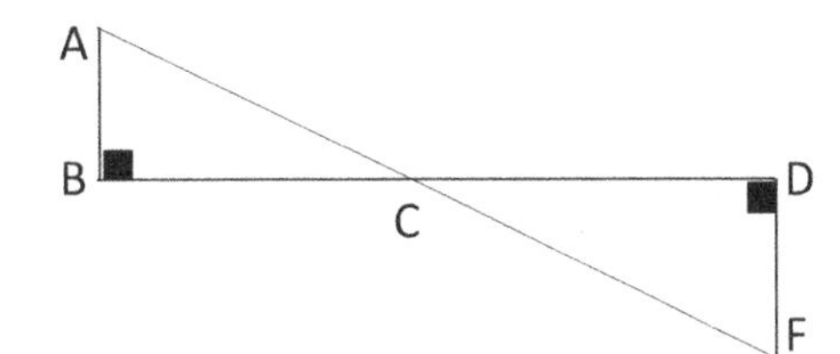

16) In the xy-plane, the point $(-2, 1)$ and $(-1, 4)$ are on the line A. Which of the following equations of lines is parallel to line A?

A. $y - x = 3$

B. $y = \frac{x}{3} + \frac{5}{3}$

C. $y = 2x + 5$

D. $2y - 6x = 5$

17) In the rectangle below if $y > 4$ cm and the area of rectangle is 40 cm^2 and the perimeter of the rectangle is 28 cm, what is the value of x and y respectively?

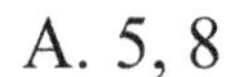
A. 5, 8

B. 4, 10

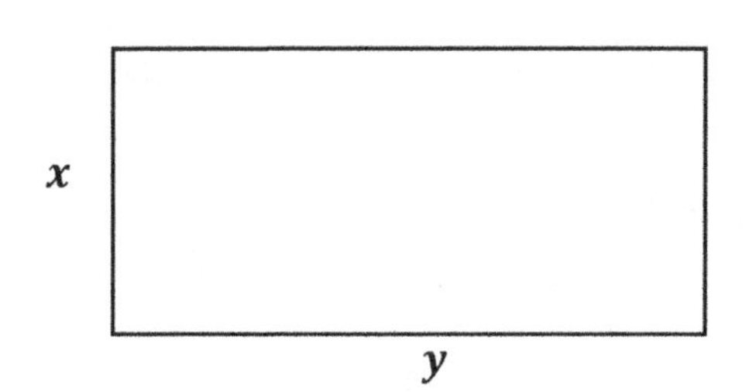

C. 2, 20

D. 1, 40

18) A football team had $25,000 to spend on supplies. The team spent $17,000 on new balls. New sport shoes cost $125 each. Which of the following inequalities represent the number of new shoes the team can purchase?

A. $125x + 8{,}000 \leq 25{,}000$

B. $125x + 17{,}000 \leq 25{,}000$

C. $17{,}000 + 125x \geq 25{,}000$

D. $8{,}000 + 125x \geq 25{,}000$

19) A $60 shirt now selling for $39 is discounted by what percent?

A. 65 %

B. 21 %

C. 54 %

D. 35 %

20) How much interest is earned on a principal of $8,000 invested at an interest rate of 2.5% for five years?

A. $2,00

B. $1,000

C. $2,000

D. $10,000

21) The price of a car was $24,000 in 2014, $18,000 in 2015 and $13,500 in 2016. What is the rate of depreciation of the price of car per year?

A. 20 %

B. 30 %

C. 25 %

D. 35 %

22) The Jackson Library is ordering some bookshelves. If x is the number of bookshelves the library wants to order, which each cost $50 and there is a one-time delivery charge of $480, which of the following represents the total cost, in dollar, per bookshelf?

A. $50x + 480$

B. $50 + 480x$

C. $\frac{50x+480}{50}$

D. $\frac{50x+480}{x}$

23) The following table represents the value of x and function $f(x)$. Which of the following could be the equation of the function $f(x)$?

x	$f(x)$
1	4
4	6
9	8
16	10

A. $f(x) = 2x^2 + 2$

B. $f(x) = x^2 + 3$

C. $f(x) = \sqrt{2x + 2}$

D. $f(x) = 2\sqrt{x} + 2$

24) The circle graph below shows all Mr. Wilson's expenses for last month. If he spent \$840 on his car, how much did he spend for his rent?

A. \$1,120

B. \$235.20

C. \$1,400

D. \$1,210

Mr. Wilson's Monthly Expenses

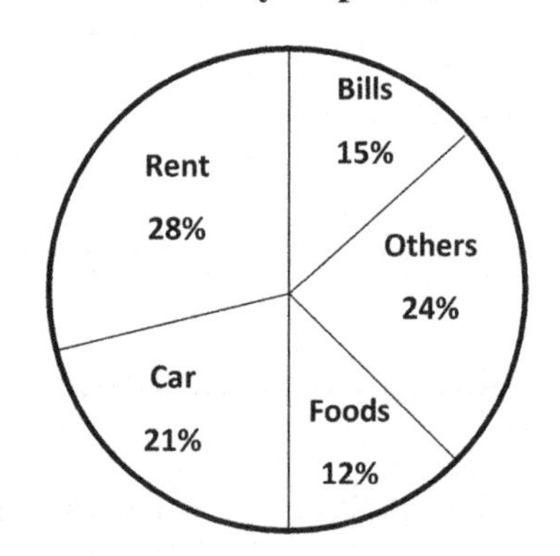

25) The sum of five different negative integers is -50. If the smallest of these integers is -12, what is the largest possible value of one of the other five integers?

A. -24

B. -12

C. -8

D. -5

26) In the following figure, point M lies on line A, what is the value of y if $x = 32$?

A. 26

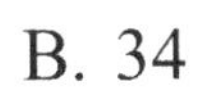
B. 34

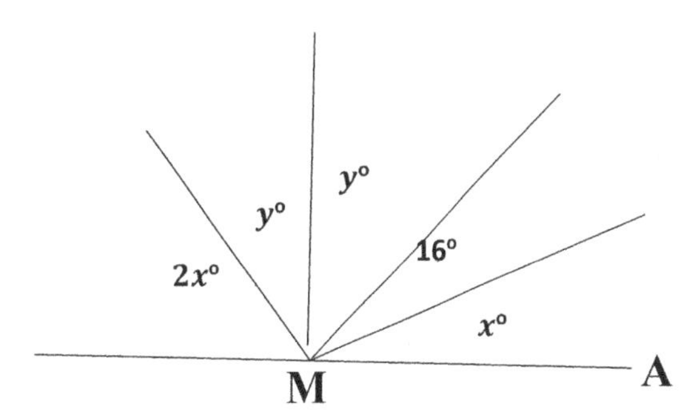

C. 36

D. 45

27) What is the smallest integer whose square root is greater than 7?

A. 49

B. 52

C. 64

D. 36

28) What is the area of the shaded region if the diameter of the bigger circle is 14 inches and the diameter of the smaller circle is 10 inches?

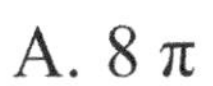
A. 8 π

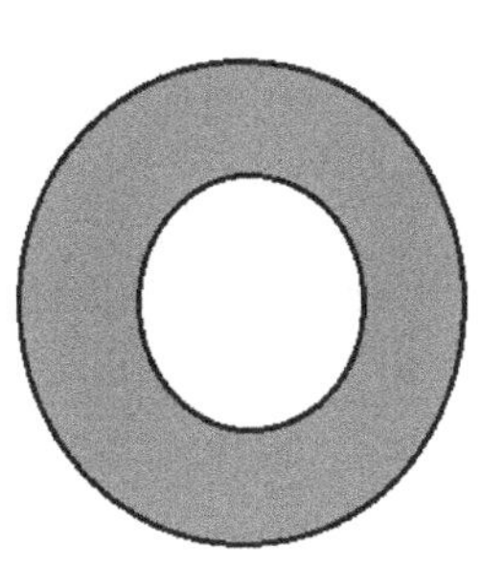

B. 16 π

C. 24 π

D. 25 π

29) What is the sum of $\sqrt{x+5}$ and $\sqrt{x} - 3$ when $\sqrt{x} = -2$?

A. -8

B. -4

C. 2

D. 0

30) What is the area of an isosceles right triangle that has one leg that measures 8 cm?

Write your answer in the box below.

31) If x is directly proportional to the square of y, and $y = 3$ when $x = 36$, then if $x = 144$ $y = ?$

A. 4

C. 8

B. 6

D. 12

32) What is the value of x in the following figure?

A. 45

B. 67

C. 68

D. 113

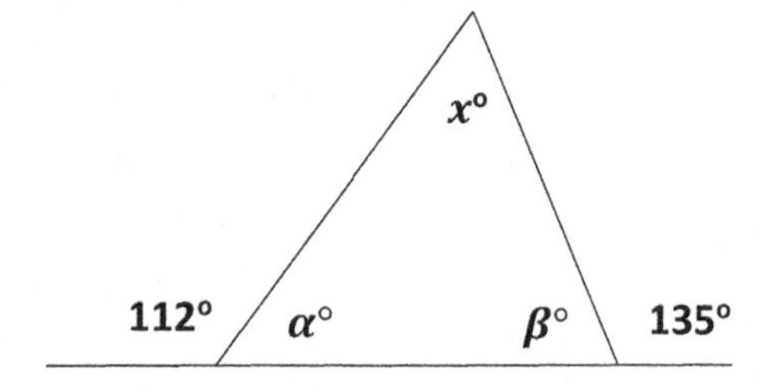

33) A swimming pool holds 1,800 cubic feet of water. The swimming pool is 24 feet long and 15 feet wide. How deep is the swimming pool?

Write your answer in the box below.

34) Jack earns \$500 for his first 40 hours of work in a week and is then paid 1.4 times his regular hourly rate for any additional hours. This week, Jack needs \$710 to pay his rent, bills and other expenses. How many hours must he work to make enough money in this week?

A. 52

B. 55

C. 12

D. 15

Questions 35, 36 and 37 are based on the following data

Types of air pollutions in 10 cities of a country

Type of Pollution	**Number of Cities**									
A										
B										
C										
D										
E										
	1	2	3	4	5	6	7	8	9	10

35) If a is the mean (average) of the number of cities in each pollution type category, b is the mode, and c is the median of the number of cities in each pollution type category, then which of the following must be true?

A. $a < b < c$

B. $b < a < c$

C. $a = c$

D. $b < c = a$

36) How many cities should be added to type of pollutions C until the ratio of cities in type of pollution C to cities in type of pollution A will be 0.750?

A. 2

B. 3

C. 4

D. 5

37) What percent of cities are in the type of pollution B, C, and E respectively?

A. 60%, 70%, 40%

B. 1.40%, 1.30%, 1.60%

C. 1.60%, 1.70%, 1.40%

D. 40%, 30%, 60%

38) In the following right triangle, if the sides AB and AC become triple longer, what will be the ratio of the perimeter of the triangle to its area?

A. $\frac{4}{3}$

B. 1

C. $\frac{1}{3}$

D. 3

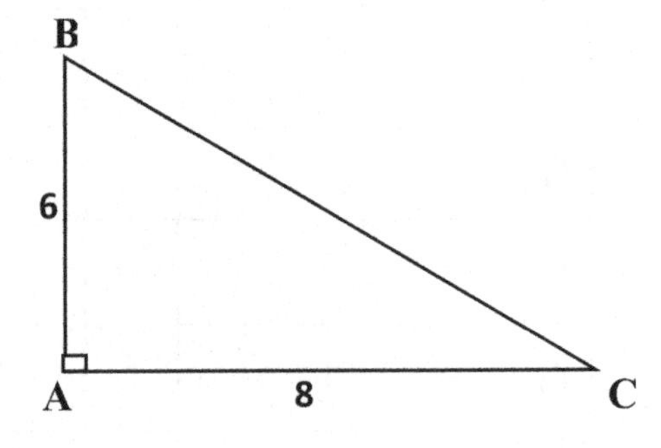

39) The capacity of a red box is 30% bigger than the capacity of a blue box. If the red box can hold 65 equal sized books, how many of the same books can the blue box hold?

A. 45

B. 50

C. 55

D. 60

40) A taxi driver earns $15 per hour work. If he works 12 hours a day, and he uses 3-liters Petrol in 2 hours with price $2.50 for 1-liter. How much money does he earn in one day?

A. $135

B. $180

C. $150

D. $65

Practice Test 2

This is the End of this Section.

State of Texas Assessments of Academic Readiness

STAAR Practice Test 3

Mathematics

GRADE 8

Administered *Month Year*

1) The area of a circle is 36 π. Which of the following can be the circumference of the circle?

A. 12 π

B. 36 π

C. 20 π

D. 16 π

2) You can buy 13 cans of green beans at a supermarket for $6.40. How much does it cost to buy 26 cans of green beans?

A. $17.78

B. $28.90

C. $12.80

D. $220.8

3) Which of the following is the solution of the following inequality?

$$8x - 4 > 18x - 9.5 - 5.5x$$

A. $x < 1$

B. $x > 1$

C. $x < -1$

D. $x > -1$

4) What is the perimeter of a square that has an area of 272.25 feet?

Write your answer in the box below.

5) A tree 14 feet tall casts a shadow 42 feet long. Jack is 6 feet tall. How long is Jack's shadow?

A. 13.25 ft

B. 16 ft

C. 18 ft

D. 42 ft

6) The price of a laptop is decreased by 20% to $345. What is its original price?

A. 431.25

B. 488.75

C. 163.75

D. 500.13

7) A container holds 5.6 gallons of water when it is $\frac{8}{44}$ full. How many gallons of water does the container hold when it's full?

A. 30.8

B. 30

C. 17.5

D. 18

8) If $(3^a)^b = 729$, then what is the value of $a \times b$?

A. $3a$

B. $3b$

C. 6

D. 3

9) A bag contains 19 balls: seven green, four black, two blue, three red and three white. If 16 balls are removed from the bag at random, what is the probability that a white ball has been removed?

A. $\frac{1}{10}$

B. $\frac{9}{25}$

C. $\frac{3}{16}$

D. $\frac{3}{25}$

10) What is the x-intercept of the line with equation $-4x + 7y = -24$?

A. -3

B. $+6$

C. $+7$

D. $-\frac{7}{24}$

11) Which of the following expressions is equivalent to

$4xy(2x - y)$?

A. $8yx^2 - 4xy$

B. $8x^2 - 4y^2$

C. $-4xy^2 + 8x^2y$

D. $4xy^2 - 8yx^2$

12) A soccer team played 120 games and won 40 percent of them. How many games did the team win?

A. 116

B. 48

C. 120

D. 51

13) The equation of a line is given as: $y = -3x + 2$. Which of the following points does not lie on the line?

A. $(-1, -2)$

B. $(1, -1)$

C. $(3, -7)$

D. $(1, 1)$

14) The perimeter of the trapezoid below is 32 cm. What is its area?

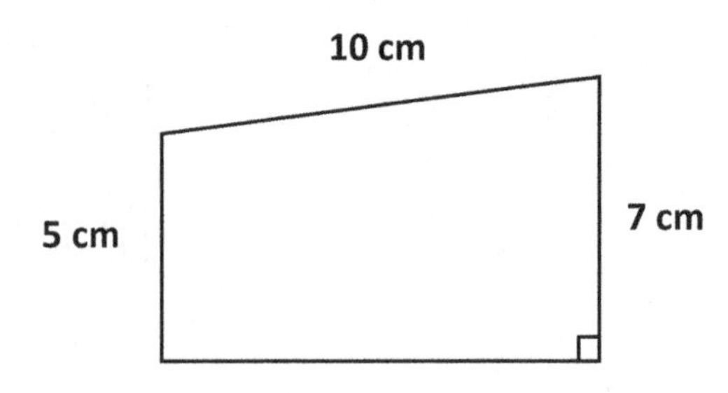

Write your answer in the box below.

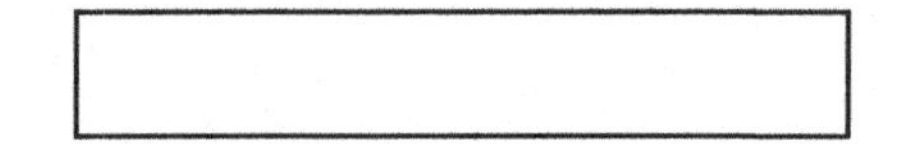

15) Which graph does not represent y as a function of x?

A.

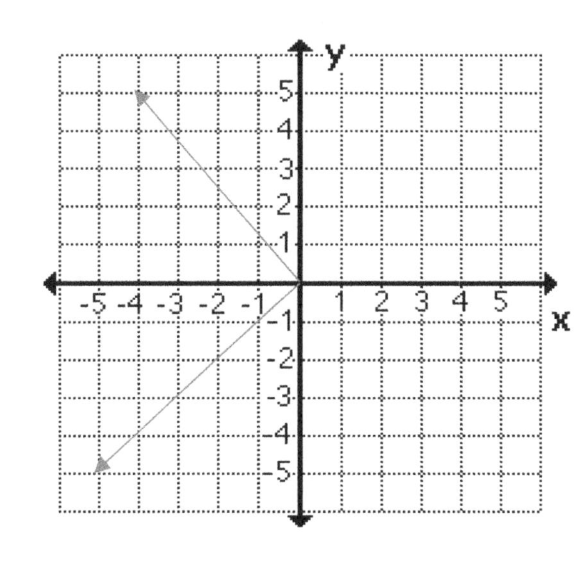

B.

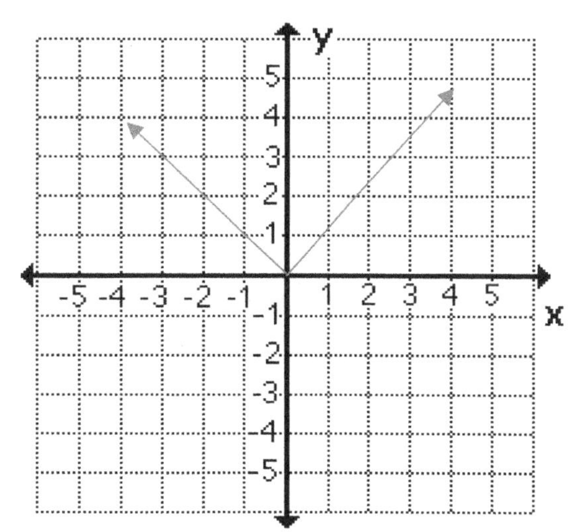

C.

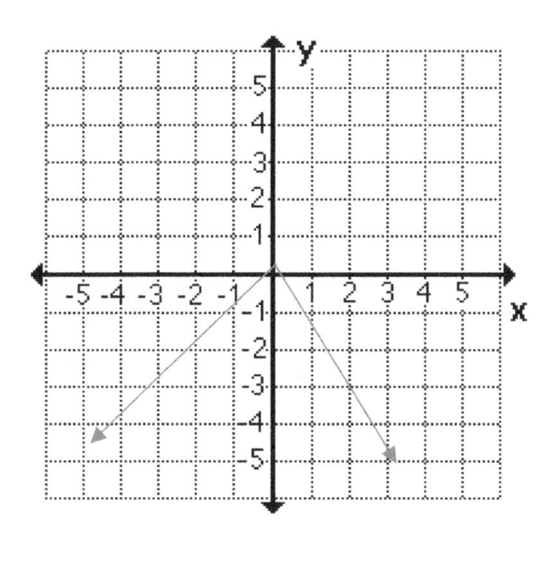

D.

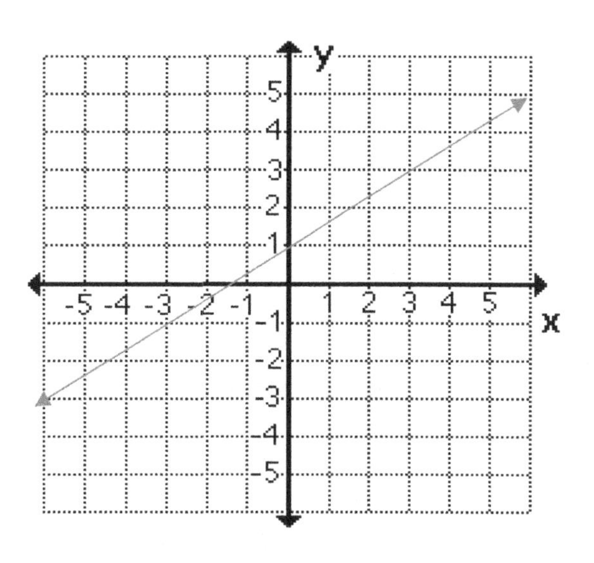

16) Which of the following is equivalent to $-21 < -4x + 3 < 3$?

A. $-6 < x < 0$

B. $0 < x < 6$

C. $6 < x < 0$

D. $-6 < x < -6$

17) A bank is offering 1.75% simple interest on a savings account. If you deposit $18,000, how much interest will you earn in four years?

A. $1,260

B. $1,640

C. $3,200

D. $1,612

18) Joe scored 20 out of 35 marks in Algebra, 48 out of 55 marks in science and 16 out of 20 marks in mathematics. In which subject his percentage of marks is best?

A. Algebra

B. Science

C. Mathematics

D. Algebra and Science

19) What is the volume of the following triangular prism?

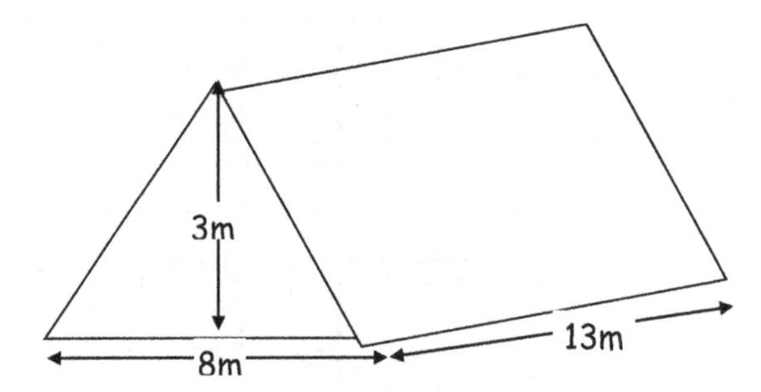

Write your answer in the box below.

20) The marked price of a computer is E Euro. Its price decreased by 20% in March and later increased by 8 % in April. What is the final price of the computer in E Euro?

A. 0.864 E

B. 0.096E

C. 0.92 E

D. 0.861 E

21) Find the slope–intercept form of the graph $3x - 6y = -18$

A. $y = 2x + \frac{2}{5}$

B. $y = \frac{1}{2}x + 3$

C. $y = \frac{1}{2}x + 3$

D. $y = \frac{1}{2}x - 3$

22) Triangle ABC is graphed on a coordinate grid with vertices at A (3, 0), B (–1, 5) and C (2, 6). Triangle ABC is reflected over x axes to create triangle A' B' C'. Which order pair represents the coordinate of C'?

A. $(6, 2)$

B. $(2, -6)$

C. $(-2, -6)$

D. $(-2, 6)$

23) Which of the following point is the solution of the system of equations?

$$\begin{cases} 2x + y = -5 \\ 3x - 2y = 10 \end{cases}$$

A. $(-5, 5)$

B. $(0, -5)$

C. $(-5, 0)$

D. $(5, -1)$

24) A shirt costing $400 is discounted 25%. After a month, the shirt is discounted another 15%. Which of the following expressions can be used to find the selling price of the shirt?

A. (400) (0.75) (0.15)

B. (400) (0.25) (0.15)

C. (400) (0.75) (.85)

D. (400) (0.25) (.85)

25) What is the distance between the points $(3, 1)$ and $(-1, -2)$?

A. 5

B. 9

C. 4

D. 3

Questions 26 and 27 are based on the following data

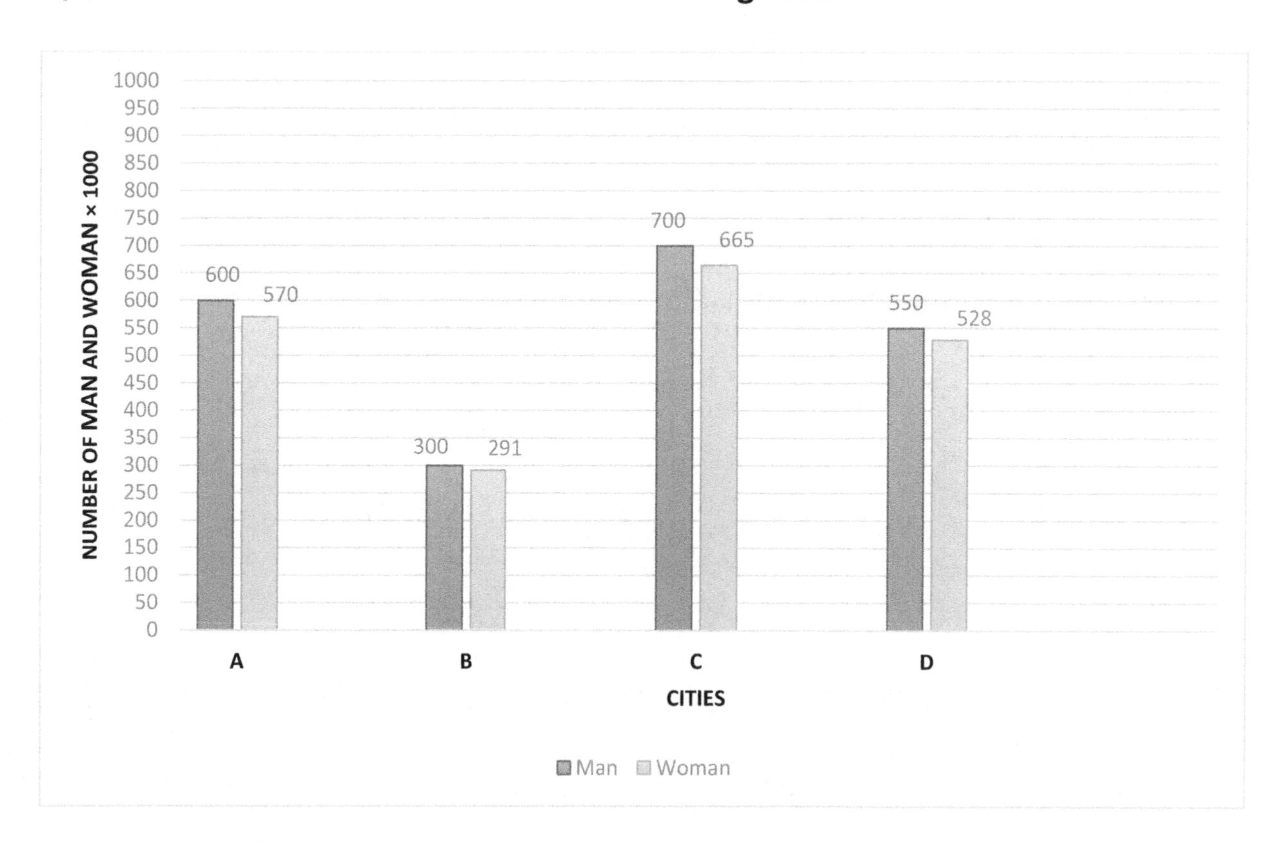

26) What's the ratio of percentage of men in city B to percentage of women in city A?

A. 0.89

B. 0.79

C. 0.96

D. 0. 91

27) What's the maximum ratio of woman to man in the four cities?

A. 0.94

B. 0.97

C. 0.96

D. 0.92

28) Line m passes through the point $(2, -5)$. Which of the following **CANNOT** be the equation of line m?

A. $y = -5$

B. $y = 3x - 11$

C. $y = -1 - x$

D. $y = -x - 3$

29) The sum of four numbers is 84. If another number is added to these four numbers, the average of the five numbers is 28. What is the fifth number?

A. 44

B. 38

C. 50

D. 56

30) David owed $14,101. After making 42 payments of $245 each, how much did he have left to pay?

A. $2,860

B. $3,120

C. $3,811

D. $2,546

31) Which of the following lines is parallel to the graph of $y = 2x - 3$?

A. $2x - 3y = 4$

B. $3x - 2y = 0$

C. $2x - y = -4$

D. $3x + y = 4$

32) The average of five consecutive numbers is 36. What is the smallest number?

A. 34

B. 38

C. 37

D. 42

33) The price of a laptop is decreased by 25% to $390. What is its original price?

A. 520

B. 428.75

C. 602.75

D. 600

34) The average weight of 18 girls in a class is 35 kg and the average weight of 22 boys in the same class is 45 kg. What is the average weight of all the 40 students in that class?

A. 45 Kg

B. 39.50 Kg

C. 44 Kg

D. 40.50 Kg

35) Liam's average (arithmetic mean) on three mathematics tests is 80. What should Liam's score be on the next test to have an overall of 78 for all the tests?

A. 72

B. 75

C. 94

D. 92

36) Which of the following equations has a graph that is a straight line?

A. $y = 3x^2 - 6$

B. $2y^2 - x^2 = 6$

C. $x - y = 6$

D. $2x + xy = 6$

37) An angle is equal to one fifth of its supplement. What is the measure of that angle?

A. 36

B. 45

C. 30

D. 60

38) One fourth of 36 is equal to $\frac{3}{5}$ of what number?

A. 32

B. 20

C. 45

D. 15

39) A card is drawn at random from a standard 52–card deck, what is the probability that the card is of Hearts? (The deck includes 13 of each suit clubs, diamonds, hearts, and spades)

A. $\frac{1}{4}$

B. $\frac{4}{13}$

C. $\frac{3}{13}$

D. $\frac{1}{13}$

40) The score of Zoe was one fifth of Emma and the score of Harper was thrice that of Emma. If the score of Harper was 90, what is the score of Zoe?

A. 12

B. 6

C. 4

D. 8

Practice Test 3

This is the End of this Section.

State of Texas Assessments of Academic Readiness

STAAR Practice Test 4

Mathematics

GRADE 8

Administered *Month Year*

1) Right triangle ABC has two legs of lengths 15 cm (AB) and 20 cm (AC). What is the length of the third side (BC)?

A. 30 cm

B. 20 cm

C. 15 cm

D. 25 cm

2) When a number is subtracted from 42 and the difference is divided by that number, the result is 6. What is the value of the number?

A. 6

B. 8

C. 9

D. 5

3) A bank is offering 1.25% simple interest on a savings account. If you deposit $8,000, how much interest will you earn in two years?

A. $540

B. $1,350

C. $440

D. $200

4) In a party, 14 soft drinks are required for every 11 guests. If there are 132 guests, how many soft drinks is required?

A. 141

B. 168

C. 175

D. 125

5) A chemical solution contains 7% alcohol. If there is 16.1 ml of alcohol, what is the volume of the solution?

A. 320 ml

B. 240 ml

C. 230 ml

D. 380 ml

6) What is the area of the shaded region?

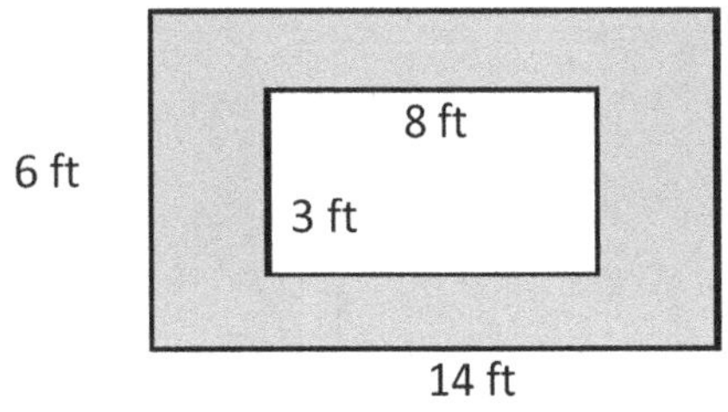

A. 60

B. 24

C. 108

D. 69

7) A rope weighs 330 grams per meter of length. What is the weight in kilograms of 15.8 meters of this rope? (1 kilograms = 1000 grams)

A. 5.63

B. 0.5214

C. 5.021

D. 5.214

8) The ratio of boys to girls in a school is 2:5. If there are 560 students in a school, how many boys are in the school.

Write your answer in the box below.

9) In two successive years, the population of a town is increased by 7% and 20%. What percent of the population is increased after two years?

A. 27%

B. 28.40%

C.

D.

10) Which graph shows a non–proportional linear relationship between x and y?

A.

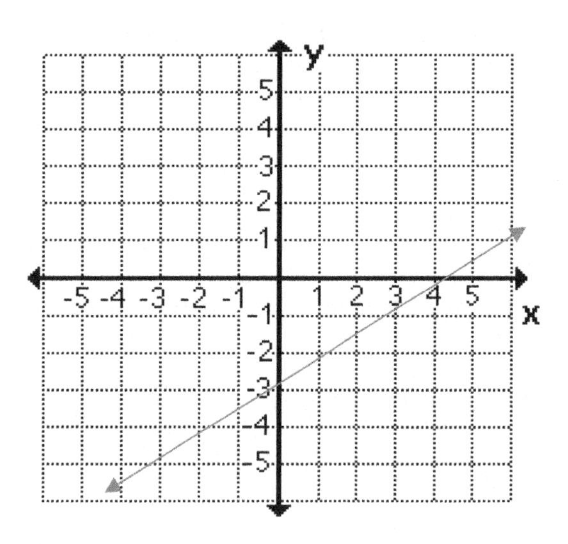

B.

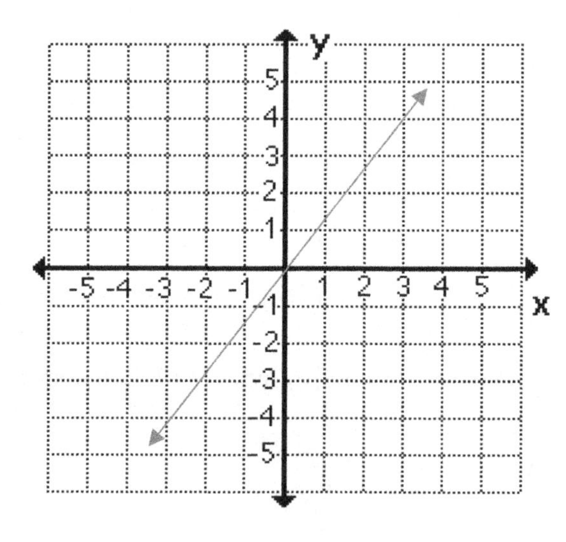

C.

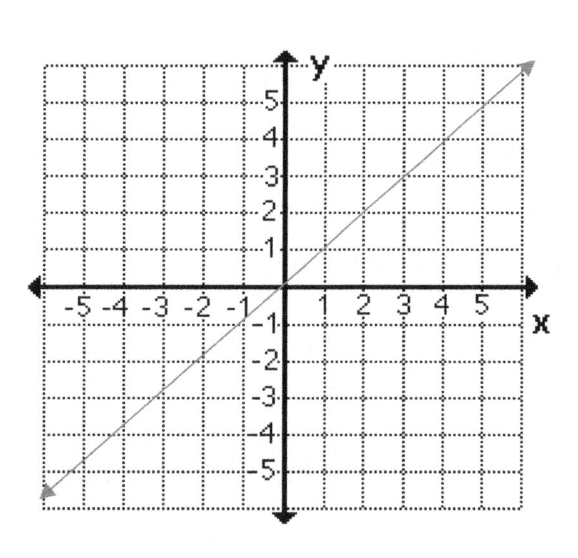

D.

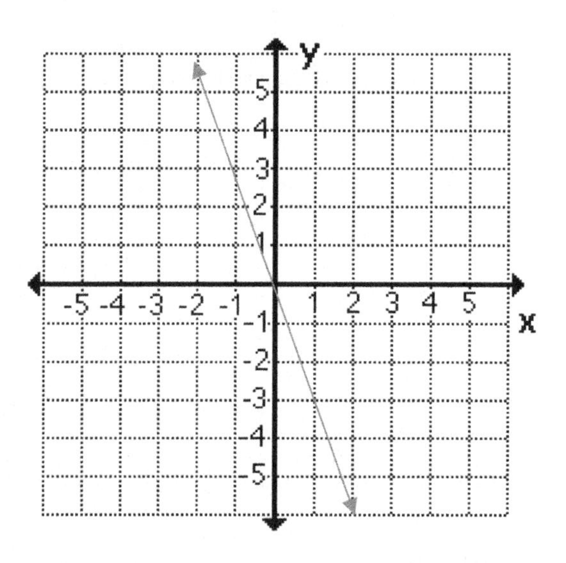

11) five years ago, Amy was five times as old as Mike was. If Mike is 10 years old now, how old is Amy?

A. 24

B. 30

C. 15

D. 23

12) What is the value of $|-20 + 11| - |8\,(-2)|$?

A. -7

C. -15

B. $+7$

D. $+19$

13) What is the solution of the following system of equations?

$$\begin{cases} \dfrac{-x}{3} + \dfrac{y}{2} = 4 \\ \dfrac{-2y}{3} + 4x = -16 \end{cases}$$

A. $x = -3\,, y = 6$

C. $x = 5\,, y = 4$

B. $x = 3\,, y = 6$

D. $x = -5, y = 4$

14) If a gas tank can hold 32 gallons, how many gallons does it contain when it is $\frac{3}{8}$ full?

A. 32.2

C. 12

B. 22.2

D. 21

15) What is the length of BC in the following figure if AB = 5, DF = 7 and BD = 36?

A. 12

B. 15

C. 24

D. 30

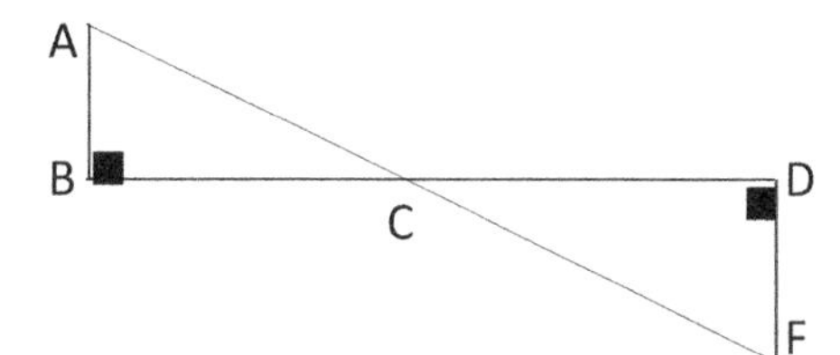

16) In the xy-plane, the point $(-3, -3)$ and $(1, 5)$ are on the line A. Which of the following equations of lines is parallel to line A?

A. $2y - x = 4$

B. $y = \frac{2x}{3} + \frac{5}{3}$

C. $2y = 3x + 6$

D. $3y - 6x = 5$

17) In the rectangle below if $y > 6$ cm and the area of rectangle is 48 cm^2 and the perimeter of the rectangle is 32 cm, what is the value of x and y respectively?

A. 4, 12

B. 4, 10

C. 4, 16

D. 12, 40

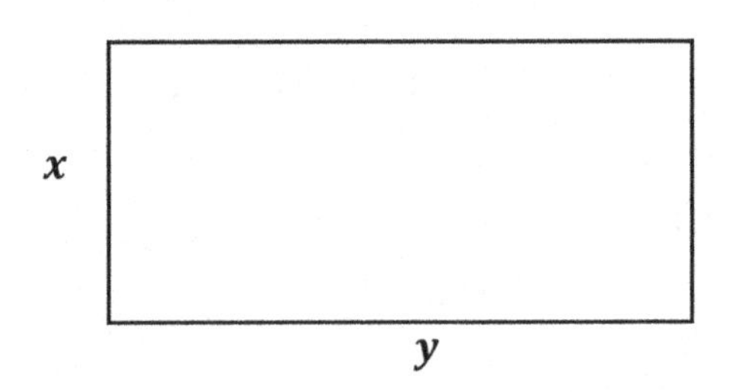

18) A football team had \$30,000 to spend on supplies. The team spent \$19,000 on new balls. New sport shoes cost \$115 each. Which of the following inequalities represent the number of new shoes the team can purchase?

A. $115x + 19{,}000 \leq 30{,}000$

B. $115x + 19{,}000 \geq 30{,}000$

C. $11{,}000 + 115x \geq 30{,}000$

D. $11{,}000 + 115x \leq 30{,}000$

19) A \$90 shirt now selling for \$45 is discounted by what percent?

A. 45 %

B. 20 %

C. 50 %

D. 55 %

20) How much interest is earned on a principal of \$10,000 invested at an interest rate of 1.5% for four years?

A. \$6,00

B. \$8,000

C. \$6,000

D. \$12,000

21) The price of a car was \$20,000 in 2014, \$16,000 in 2015 and \$12,800 in 2016. What is the rate of depreciation of the price of car per year?

A. 20 %

B. 40 %

C. 25 %

D. 45 %

22) The Jackson Library is ordering some bookshelves. If x is the number of bookshelves the library wants to order, which each cost \$65 and there is a one-time delivery charge of \$540, which of the following represents the total cost, in dollar, per bookshelf?

A. $65x + 540$

B. $65 + 540x$

C. $\frac{65x+540}{65}$

D. $\frac{65x+540}{x}$

23) The following table represents the value of x and function $f(x)$. Which of the following could be the equation of the function $f(x)$?

x	$f(x)$
1	1
4	16
9	81
10	100

A. $f(x) = x^2 + 2$

B. $f(x) = x^2$

C. $f(x) = \sqrt{x+5}$

D. $f(x) = 2\sqrt{x} + 2$

24) The circle graph below shows all Mr. Wilson's expenses for last month. If he spent \$720 on his car, how much did he spend for his rent?

A. \$9,120

B. \$936

C. \$9,400

D. 2,110

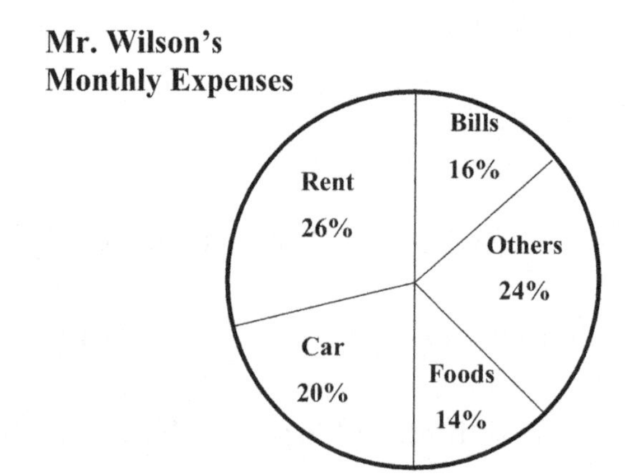

25) The sum of four different negative integers is -34. If the smallest of these integers is -10, what is the largest possible value of one of the other four integers?

A. -7

B. -9

C. -8

D. -15

26) In the following figure, point M lies on the line A, what is the value of y if $x = 28$?

A. 36

B. 44

C. 41

D. 30

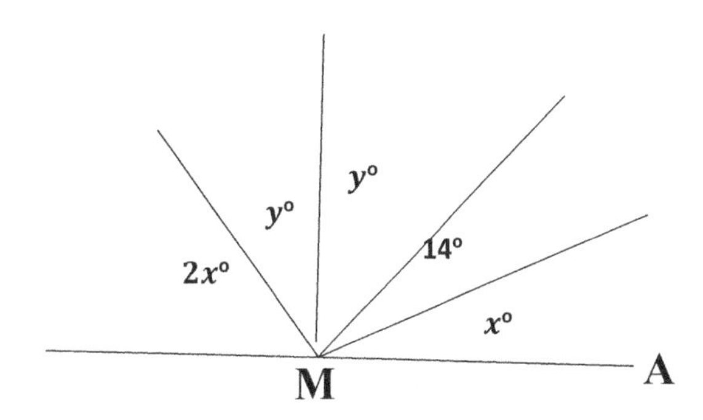

27) What is the smallest integer whose square root is greater than 6?

A. 51

B. 25

C. 64

D. 40

28) What is the area of the shaded region if the diameter of the bigger circle is 12 inches and the diameter of the smaller circle is 8 inches?

A. 18 π

B. 26 π

C. 20π

D. 25 π

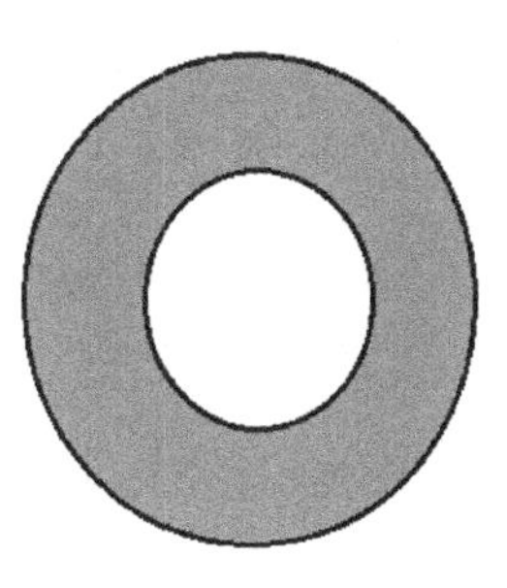

29) What is the sum of $\sqrt{x+7}$ and $\sqrt{x} - 2$ when $\sqrt{x} = -3$?

A. -5

B. -3

C. 2

D. 5

30) What is the area of an isosceles right triangle that has one leg that measures 12 cm?

Write your answer in the box below.

31) If x is directly proportional to the square of y, and $y = 2$ when $x = 32$, then if $x = 128$ $y = ?$

A. 4

C. 8

B. 16

D. 22

32) What is the value of x in the following figure?

A. 55

B. 65

C. 75

D. 105

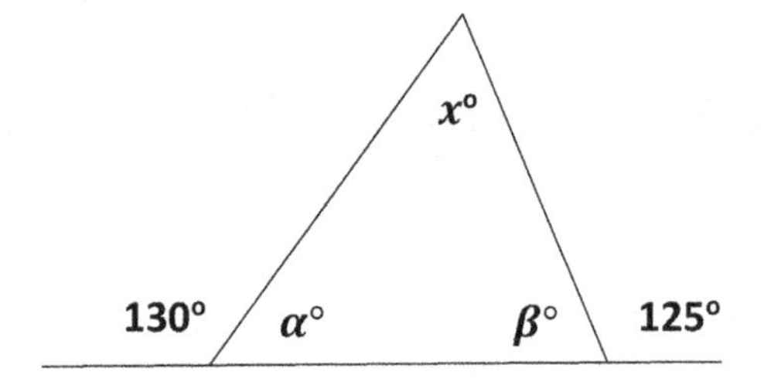

33) A swimming pool holds 1,248 cubic feet of water. The swimming pool is 26 feet long and 12 feet wide. How deep is the swimming pool?

Write your answer in the box below.

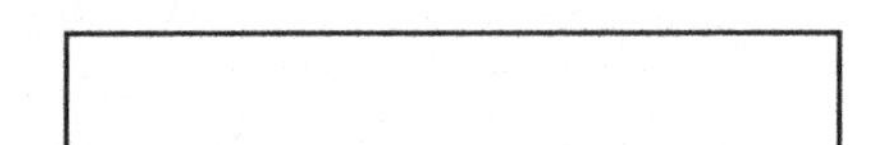

34) Jack earns $600 for his first 30 hours of work in a week and is then paid 2 times his regular hourly rate for any additional hours. This week, Jack needs $1,120 to pay his rent, bills and other expenses. How many hours must he work to make enough money in this week?

A. 42

C. 43

B. 45

D. 25

Questions 35, 36 and 37 are based on the following data

Types of air pollutions in 10 cities of a country

Type of Pollution	**Number of Cities**									
A	■	■	■	■	■	■	■	■		
B	■	■	■	■						
C	■	■	■							
D	■	■	■	■	■	■	■	■	■	■
E	■	■	■	■	■					
	1	2	3	4	5	6	7	8	9	10

35) If a is the mean (average) of the number of cities in each pollution type category, b is the mode, and c is the median of the number of cities in each pollution type category, then which of the following must be true?

A. $a < b < c$

C. $c < a$

B. $b < a < c$

D. $b < c = a$

36) How many cities should be added to type of pollutions B until the ratio of cities in type of pollution B to cities in type of pollution D will be 0.80?

A. 6

C. 8

B. 4

D. 5

37) What percent of cities are in the type of pollution A, C, and E respectively?

A. 80%, 30%, 50%

C. 1.30%, 1.70%, 1.40%

B. 1.80%, 1.30%, 1.50%

D. 40%, 30%, 60%

38) In the following right triangle, if the sides AB and AC become double longer, what will be the ratio of the perimeter of the triangle to its area?

A. $\frac{4}{3}$

B. 2

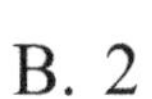

C. $\frac{1}{3}$

D. 4

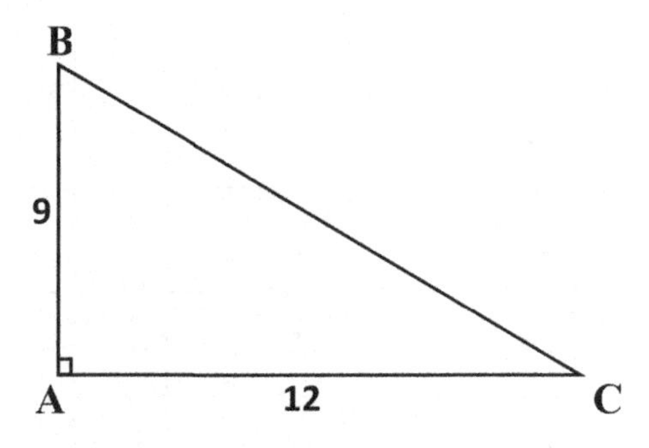

39) The capacity of a red box is 20% bigger than the capacity of a blue box. If the red box can hold 84 equal sized books, how many of the same books can the blue box hold?

A. 75

C. 70

B. 40

D. 60

40) A taxi driver earns $14 per hour work. If he works 8 hours a day, and he uses 4-liters Petrol in 2 hours with price $1.75 for 1-liter. How much money does he earn in one day?

A. $115

B. $120

C. $112

D. $84

Practice Test 4

This is the End of this Section.

State of Texas Assessments of Academic Readiness

STAAR Practice Test 5

Mathematics

GRADE 8

Administered *Month Year*

1) The area of a circle is 49π. Which of the following can be the circumference of the circle?

A. $14\ \pi$

B. $18\ \pi$

C. $24\ \pi$

D. $12\ \pi$

2) You can buy 14 cans of green beans at a supermarket for $3.80. How much does it cost to buy 52 cans of green beans?

A. $14.88

B. $24.56

C. $14.11

D. $114.1

3) Which of the following is the solution of the following inequality?

$$-9x + 25.5 > -12x + 14.5 + 8.5x$$

A. $x < 2$

B. $x > 2$

C. $x < -2$

D. $x > -2$

4) What is the perimeter of a square that has an area of 302.76 feet?

Write your answer in the box below.

5) A tree 16 feet tall casts a shadow 34 feet long. Jack is 8 feet tall. How long is Jack's shadow?

A. 19 ft

B. 21 ft

C. 17 ft

D. 36 ft

6) The price of a laptop is decreased by 35% to $580. What is its original price?

A. 892.30

B. 829.30

C. 280.9

D. 920.8

7) A container holds 4.8 gallons of water when it is $\frac{8}{41}$ full. How many gallons of water does the container hold when it's full?

A. 24.6

B. 34

C. 14.45

D. 8.42

8) If $(4^a)^b = 256$, then what is the value of $a \times b$?

A. $4a$

B. $5b$

C. 4

D. 5

9) A bag contains 20 balls: seven green, two black, two blue, eight red and one white. If 18 balls are removed from the bag at random, what is the probability that a white ball has been removed?

A. $\frac{3}{20}$

B. $\frac{18}{20}$

C. $\frac{1}{20}$

D. $\frac{1}{18}$

10) What is the x-intercept of the line with equation $-9x + 5y = 63$?

A. -5

B. -7

C. $+9$

D. $-\frac{9}{5}$

11) Which of the following expressions is equivalent to

$$8x^3y(3x + 2y)?$$

A. $24yx^2 - 16x^3y$

C. $24yx^4 + 16x^3y^2$

B. $24x^2 - 16y^2$

D. $24x^3y^2 - 16yx^2$

12) A soccer team played 150 games and won 30 percent of them. How many games did the team win?

A. 110

C. 95

B. 45

D. 70

13) The equation of a line is given as: $y = -2x + 5$. Which of the following points does not lie on the line?

A. $(4, -3)$

C. $(-1, 7)$

B. $(1, 3)$

D. $(1, -1)$

14) The perimeter of the trapezoid below is 28 cm. What is its area?

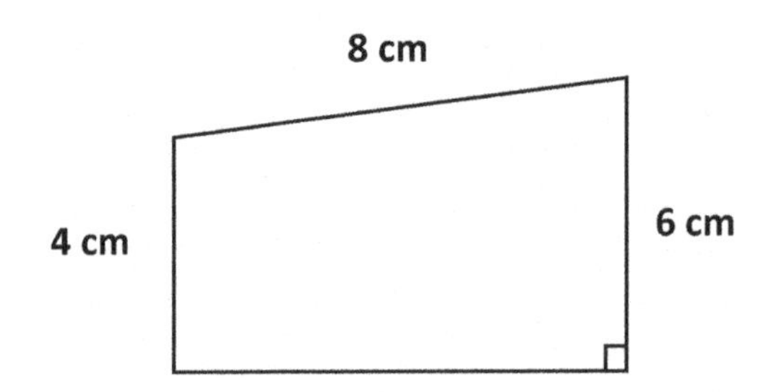

Write your answer in the box below.

15) Which graph does not represent y as a function of x?

A.

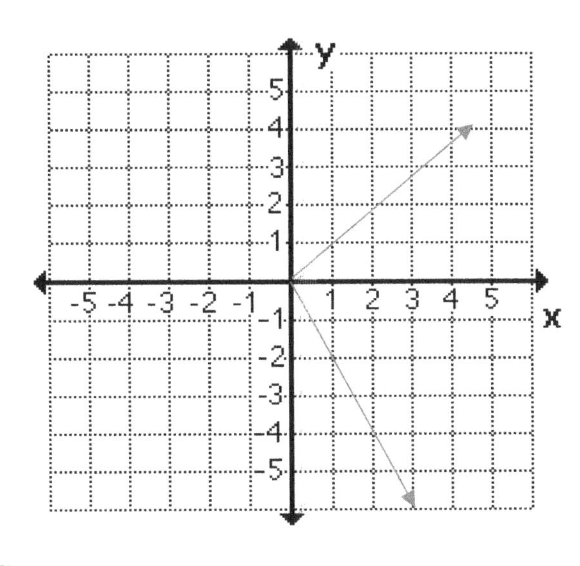

B.

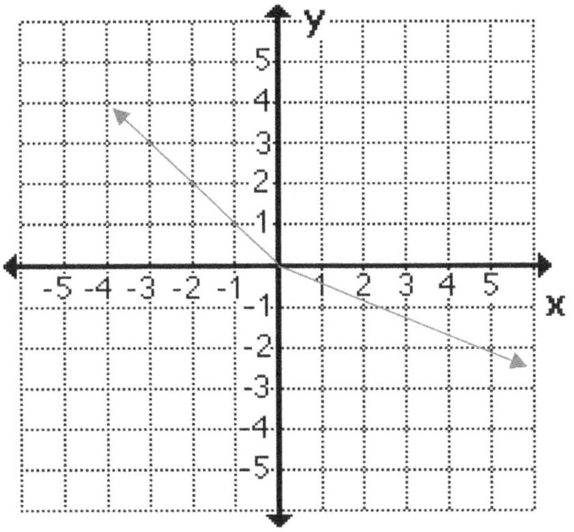

C.

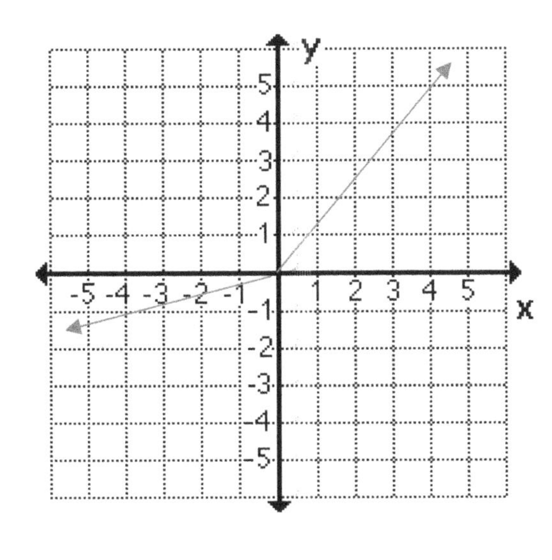

D.

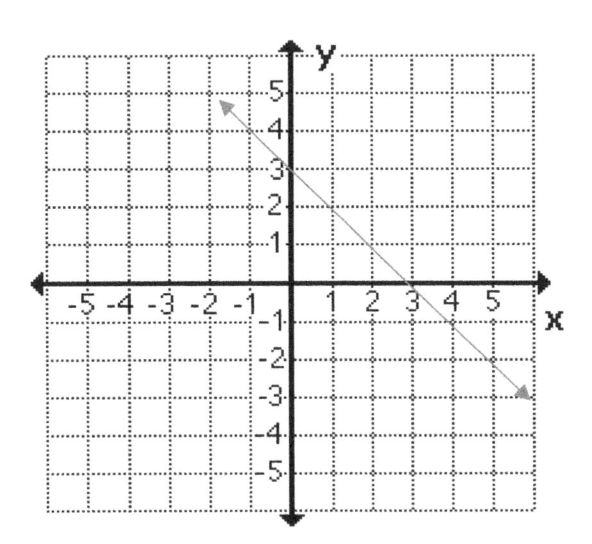

16) Which of the following is equivalent to $-43 < -7x + 6 < 6$?

A. $0 < x < 7$

B. $1 < x < 7$

C. $-7 < x < 0$

D. $-7 < x < 7$

17) A bank is offering 2.25% simple interest on a savings account. If you deposit \$22,000, how much interest will you earn in five years?

A. \$2,475

B. \$1,750

C. \$2,780

D. \$4,840

18) Joe scored 34 out of 48 marks in Algebra, 26 out of 32 marks in science and 15 out of 22 marks in mathematics. In which subject his percentage of marks is best?

A. Mathematics

B. Science

C. Algebra

D. Mathematics and Science

19) What is the volume of the following triangular prism?

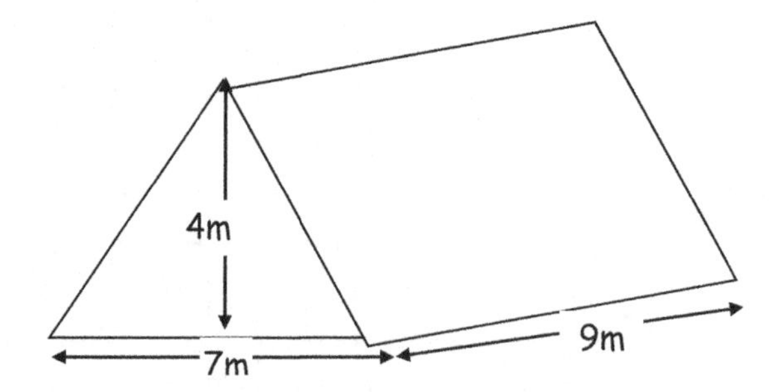

Write your answer in the box below.

20) The marked price of a computer is E Euro. Its price decreased by 22% in March and later increased by 5 % in April. What is the final price of the computer in E Euro?

A. 0.819 E

B. 0.098E

C. 0.81 E

D. 0.918 E

21) Find the slope–intercept form of the graph $2x - 4y = 16$

A. $y = 2x + 4$

B. $y = -\frac{1}{2}x + 4$

C. $y = \frac{1}{2}x - 4$

D. $y = -\frac{1}{2}x - 4$

22) Triangle ABC is graphed on a coordinate grid with vertices at A (4, 2), B (–3, 7) and C (1, 8). Triangle ABC is reflected over x axes to create triangle A' B' C'. Which order pair represents the coordinate of C'?

A. $(8, 1)$

B. $(1, -8)$

C. $(-1, -8)$

D. $(-1, 8)$

23) Which of the following point is the solution of the system of equations?

$$\begin{cases} 5x - 4y = 13 \\ 2x + 3y = -4 \end{cases}$$

A. $(-2, 1)$

B. $(1, -2)$

C. $(-2, 2)$

D. $(2, -2)$

24) A shirt costing $700 is discounted 30%. After a month, the shirt is discounted another 12%. Which of the following expressions can be used to find the selling price of the shirt?

A. (700) (0.70) (0.12)

B. (700) (0.30) (0.12)

C. (700) (0.70) (0.88)

D. (700) (0.30) (0.88)

25) What is the distance between the points $(4, 2)$ and $(-8, -3)$?

A. 13

B. 11

C. 14

D. 15

Questions 26 and 27 are based on the following data

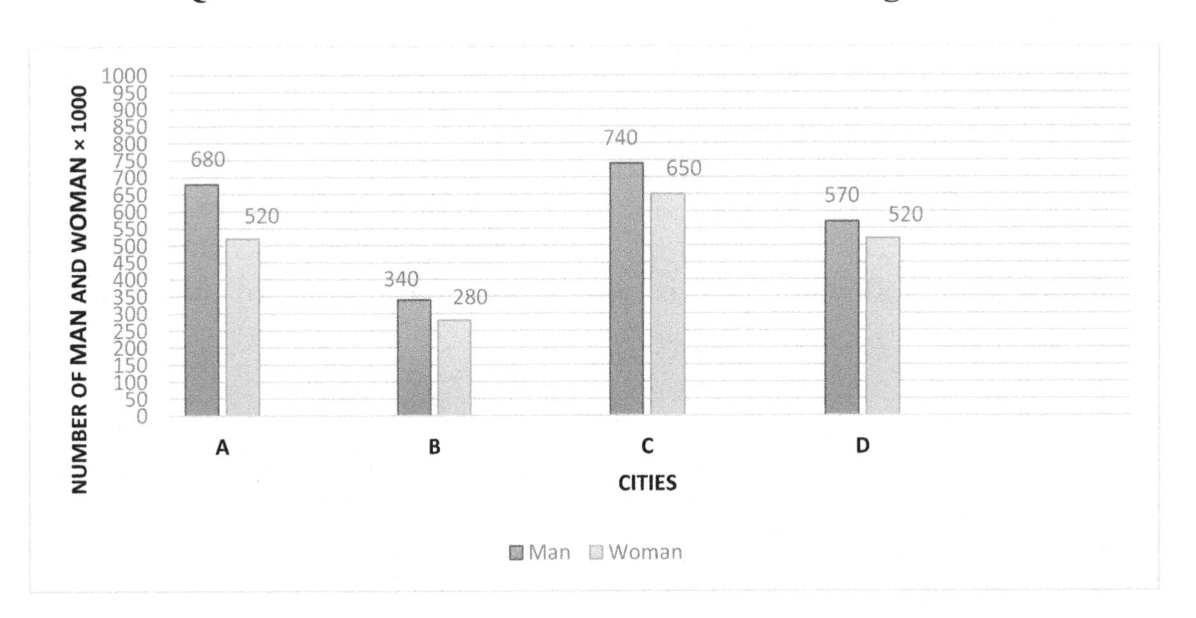

26) What's the ratio of percentage of men in city C to percentage of women in city B?

A. 0.099

B. 0.809

C. 1.18

D. 1.01

27) What's the maximum ratio of woman to man in the four cities?

A. 0.90

B. 0.91

C. 0.87

D. 0.97

28) Line m passes through the point $(4, -7)$. Which of the following **CANNOT** be the equation of line m?

A. $y = -7$

C. $y = -2 + x$

B. $y = -2x + 1$

D. $y = -3x + 5$

29) The sum of five numbers is 98. If another number is added to these five numbers, the average of the six numbers is 32. What is the sixth number?

A. 102

C. 88

B. 92

D. 94

30) David owed $15,435. After making 38 payments of $324 each, how much did he have left to pay?

A. $3,382

C. $3,123

B. $4,231

D. $4,301

31) Which of the following lines is parallel to the graph of $y = 8x - 5$?

A. $8x - 2y = 5$

C. $8x - y = -11$

B. $4x - 3y = 8$

D. $4x + y = 10$

32) The average of six consecutive numbers is 22.5. What is the smallest number?

A. 20

C. 23

B. 19

D. 21

33) The price of a laptop is decreased by 16% to $378. What is its original price?

A. 450

B. 410.5

C. 840

D. 240

34) The average weight of 16 girls in a class is 40 kg and the average weight of 29 boys in the same class is 50 kg. What is the average weight of all the 45 students in that class?

A. 40.56 Kg

B. 42.56Kg

C. 46.88 Kg

D. 46.44 Kg

35) Liam's average (arithmetic mean) on four mathematics tests is 76. What should Liam's score be on the next test to have an overall of 72 for all the tests?

A. 56

B. 58

C. 68

D. 70

36) Which of the following equations has a graph that is a straight line?

A. $y = 2x^2 - 7$

B. $5y^2 - 3x^2 = 7$

C. $x - y = 8$

D. $3x + xy = 8$

37) An angle is equal to one seventh of its supplement. What is the measure of that angle?

A. 26

B. 18

C. 22.5

D. 24.5

38) Two ninth of 27 is equal to $\frac{6}{11}$ of what number?

A. 36

B. 22

C. 44

D. 11

39) A card is drawn at random from a standard 52–card deck, what is the probability that the card is of Hearts or diamonds? (The deck includes 13 of each suit clubs, diamonds, hearts, and spades)

A. $\frac{1}{2}$

B. $\frac{2}{13}$

C. $\frac{2}{52}$

D. $\frac{3}{13}$

40) The score of Zoe was one sixth of Emma and the score of Harper was twice that of Emma. If the score of Harper was 84, what is the score of Zoe?

A. 14

B. 7

C. 16

D. 9

Practice Test 5

This is the End of this Section.

State of Texas Assessments of Academic Readiness

STAAR Practice Test 6

Mathematics

GRADE 8

Administered *Month Year*

1) Right triangle ABC has two legs of lengths 18 cm (AB) and 24 cm (AC). What is the length of the third side (BC)?

A. 15 cm

B. 28 cm

C. 42 cm

D. 30 cm

2) When a number is subtracted from 80 and the difference is divided by that number, the result is 4. What is the value of the number?

A. 16

B. 20

C. 18

D. 12

3) A bank is offering 2.4% simple interest on a savings account. If you deposit $10,000, how much interest will you earn in three years?

A. $140

B. $1,540

C. $360

D. $720

4) In a party, 15 soft drinks are required for every 9 guests. If there are 162 guests, how many soft drinks is required?

A. 135

B. 270

C. 180

D. 320

5) A chemical solution contains 16% alcohol. If there is 9.2 ml of alcohol, what is the volume of the solution?

A. 57.5ml

B. 435 ml

C. 575 ml

D. 685 ml

6) What is the area of the shaded region?

A. 72

B. 112

C. 40

D. 86

7) A rope weighs 210 grams per meter of length. What is the weight in kilograms of 22.3 meters of this rope? (1 kilograms = 1000 grams)

A. 4,683

B. 0.4683

C. 46.83

D. 4.683

8) The ratio of boys to girls in a school is 5: 9. If there are 364 students in a school, how many boys are in the school.

Write your answer in the box below.

9) In two successive years, the population of a town is increased by 8% and 14%. What percent of the population is increased after two years?

A. 26.1%

B. 23.12%

C. 123.12%

D. 45.6 %

10) Which graph shows a non–proportional linear relationship between x and y?

A.

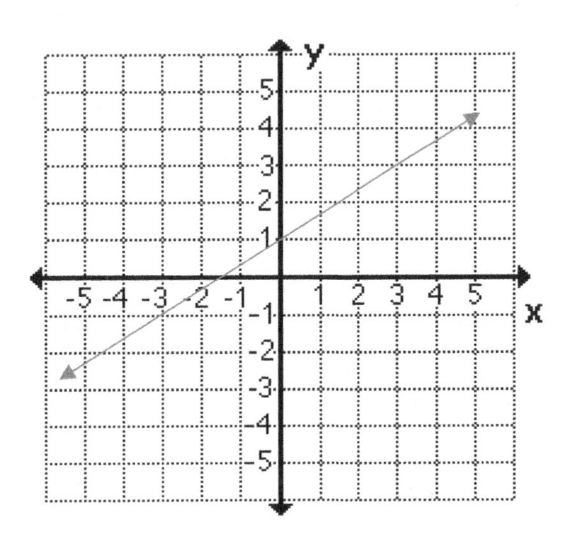

B.

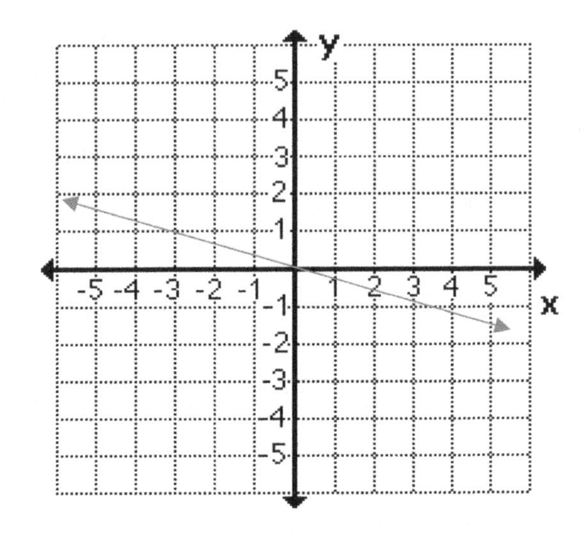

C.

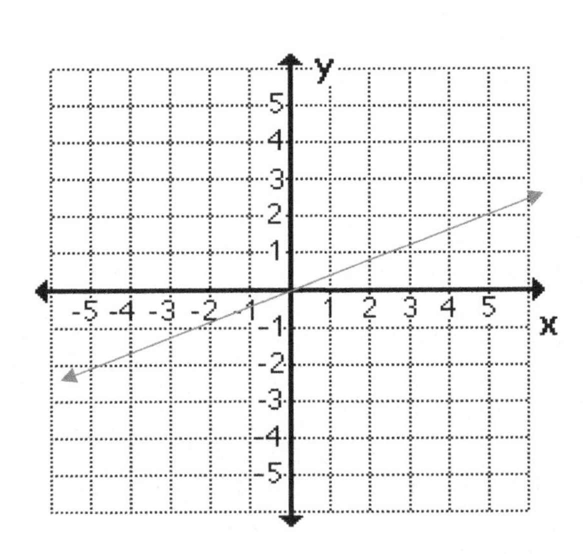

D.

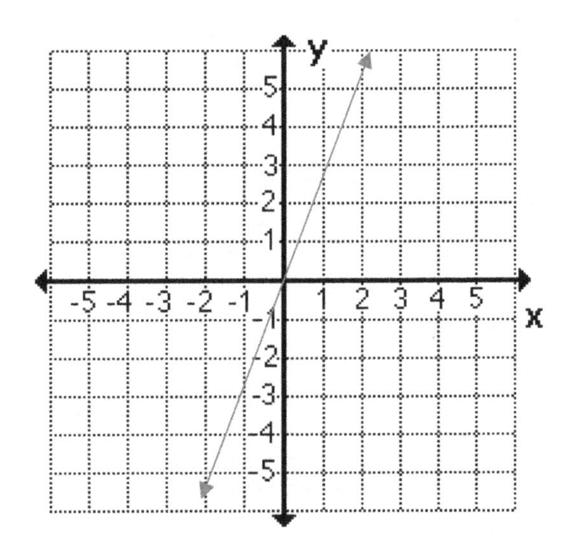

11) Four years ago, Amy was three times as old as Mike was. If Mike is 12 years old now, how old is Amy?

A. 18

B. 28

C. 36

D. 24

12) What is the value of $|-44+15|-|6\,(-3)|$?

A. 11

B. -11

C. -13

D. $+13$

13) What is the solution of the following system of equations?

$$\begin{cases} \dfrac{x}{6}+\dfrac{y}{4}=2 \\ \dfrac{-5y}{6}-2x=-11 \end{cases}$$

A. $x=3\,,y=6$

B. $x=2\,,y=8$

C. $x=4\,,y=8$

D. $x=-6,y=8$

14) If a gas tank can hold 45 gallons, how many gallons does it contain when it is $\frac{2}{9}$ full?

A. 42

B. 30

C. 10

D. 20

15) What is the length of BC in the following figure if AB = 3, DF = 4 and BD = 42?

A. 14

B. 18

C. 9

D. 36

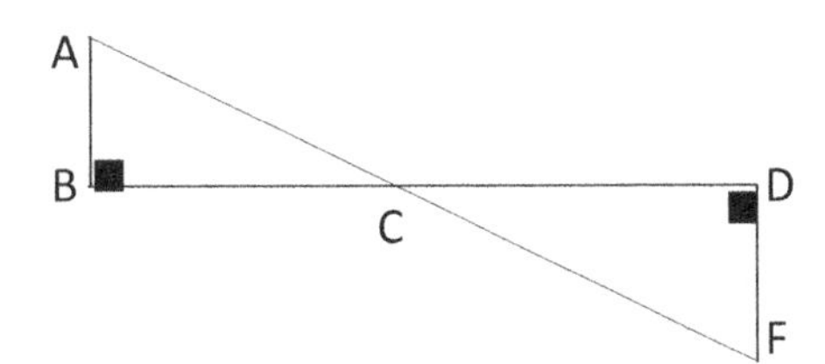

16) In the xy-plane, the point $(3, 2)$ and $(5, 8)$ are on the line A. Which of the following equations of lines is parallel to line A?

A. $4y - 3x = 5$

B. $y = \frac{3x}{5} + \frac{7}{5}$

C. $3y = 2x + 8$

D. $4y - 12x = 7$

17) In the rectangle below if $y > 9$ cm and the area of rectangle is 90 cm^2 and the perimeter of the rectangle is 38 cm, what is the value of x and y respectively?

A. 9, 10

B. 7, 12

C. 12, 7

D. 5, 18

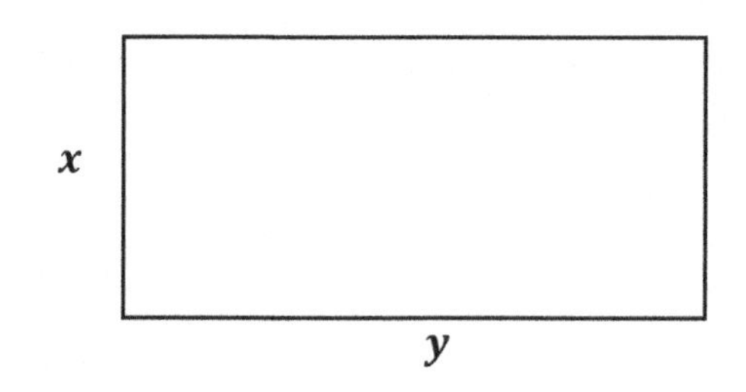

18) A football team had $26,000 to spend on supplies. The team spent $18,000 on new balls. New sport shoes cost $102 each. Which of the following inequalities represent the number of new shoes the team can purchase?

A. $102x + 18{,}000 \leq 26{,}000$

B. $102x + 18{,}000 \geq 26{,}000$

C. $18{,}000 + 102x \geq 26{,}000$

D. $18{,}000 + 102x \leq 26{,}000$

19) A \$70 shirt now selling for \$49 is discounted by what percent?

A. 55 %

B. 40 %

C. 30 %

D. 35 %

20) How much interest is earned on a principal of \$11,000 invested at an interest rate of 2.5% for six years?

A. \$1,650

B. \$2,400

C. \$1,880

D. \$16,560

21) The price of a car was \$56,000 in 2014, \$42,000 in 2015 and \$31,500 in 2016. What is the rate of depreciation of the price of car per year?

A. 25 %

B. 10 %

C. 35 %

D. 55 %

22) The Jackson Library is ordering some bookshelves. If x is the number of bookshelves the library wants to order, which each cost \$86 and there is a one-time delivery charge of \$670, which of the following represents the total cost, in dollar, per bookshelf?

A. $86x + 670$

B. $86 + 670x$

C. $\frac{86x+670}{86}$

D. $\frac{86x+670}{x}$

23) The following table represents the value of x and function $f(x)$. Which of the following could be the equation of the function $f(x)$?

x	$f(x)$
0	6
2	10
8	14
32	22

A. $f(x) = 2x^2 + 6$

B. $f(x) = 4x^2 - 6x + 6$

C. $f(x) = \sqrt{2x + 6}$

D. $f(x) = 2\sqrt{2x} + 6$

24) The circle graph below shows all Mr. Wilson's expenses for last month. If he spent $880 on his car, how much did he spend for his rent?

A. $1,720

B. $1,360

C. $4,000

D. 2,620

Mr. Wilson's Monthly Expenses

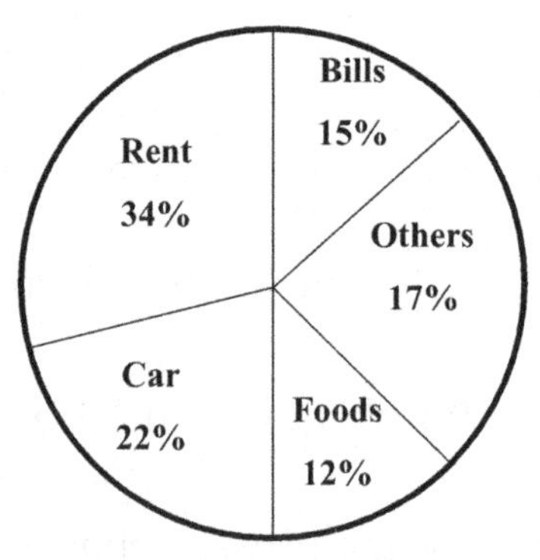

25) The sum of five different negative integers is -50. If the smallest of these integers is -12, what is the largest possible value of one of the other five integers?

A. -8

B. -4

C. -6

D. -12

26) In the following figure, point M lies on the line A, what is the value of y if $x = 10$?

A. 16

B. 38

C. 19

D. 40

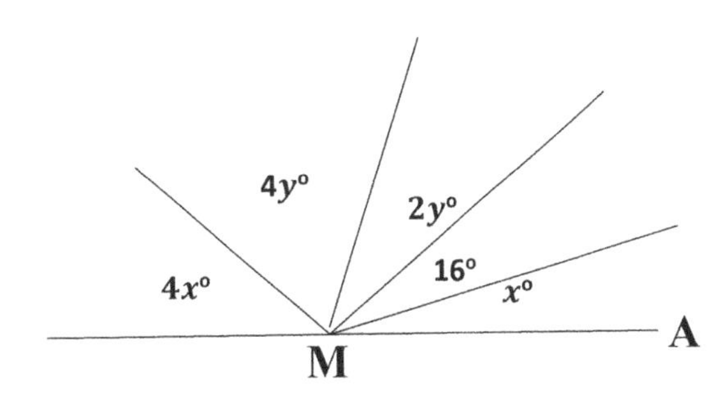

27) What is the smallest integer whose square root is greater than 7?

A. 121

B. 52

C. 81

D. 58

28) What is the area of the shaded region if the diameter of the bigger circle is 10 inches and the diameter of the smaller circle is 6 inches?

A. 30 π

B. 24 π

C. 16π

D. 12 π

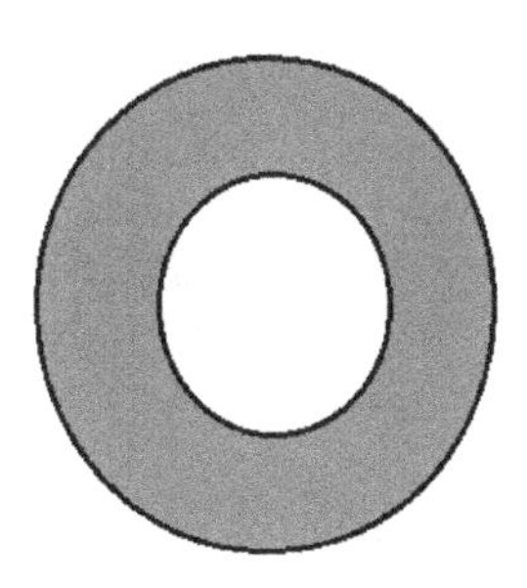

29) What is the sum of $\sqrt{3x+6}$ and $\sqrt{x} - 4$ when $\sqrt{x} = -5$?

A. −9

B. −6

C. 8

D. 10

30) What is the area of an isosceles right triangle that has one leg that measures 14 cm?

Write your answer in the box below.

31) If x is directly proportional to the square of y, and $y = 3$ when $x = 63$, then if $x = 175$ $y = ?$

A. 5

B. 10

C. 12

D. 25

32) What is the value of x in the following figure?

A. 50

B. 70

C. 60

D. 100

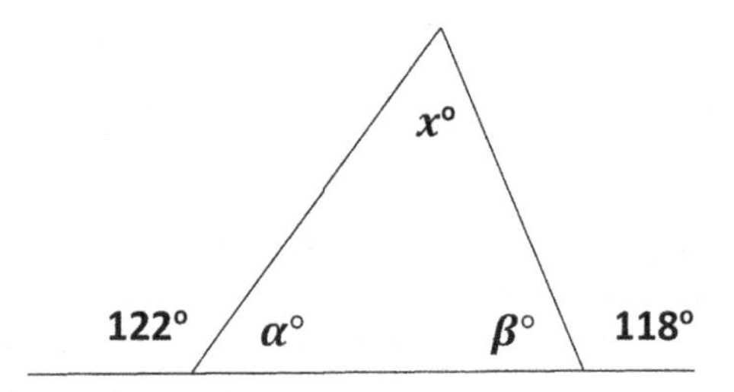

33) A swimming pool holds 1,344 cubic feet of water. The swimming pool is 32 feet long and 14 feet wide. How deep is the swimming pool?

Write your answer in the box below.

34) Jack earns \$500 for his first 25 hours of work in a week and is then paid 1.5 times his regular hourly rate for any additional hours. This week, Jack needs \$920 to pay his rent, bills and other expenses. How many hours must he work to make enough money in this week?

A. 46

B. 48

C. 34

D. 36

<u>Questions 35, 36 and 37 are based on the following data</u>

Types of air pollutions in 10 cities of a country

Type of Pollution	**Number of Cities**									
A										
B										
C										
D										
E										
	1	2	3	4	5	6	7	8	9	10

35) If a is the mean (average) of the number of cities in each pollution type category, b is the mode, and c is the median of the number of cities in each pollution type category, then which of the following must be true?

A. $a = b < c$

B. $b = a = c$

C. $c < a$

D. $b < c < a$

36) How many cities should be added to type of pollutions B until the ratio of cities in type of pollution B to cities in type of pollution D will be 1?

A. 3

B. 6

C. 9

D. 12

37) What percent of cities are in the type of pollution A, C, and E respectively?

A. 60%, 20%, 40%

B. 1.60%, 1.20%, 1.40%

C. 1.40%, 1.60%, 1.70%

D. 20%, 50%, 80%

38) In the following right triangle, if the sides AB and AC become half longer, what will be the ratio of the perimeter of the triangle to its area?

A. 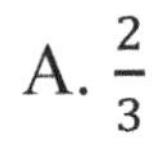

B. $\frac{1}{2}$

C. 2

D. 1

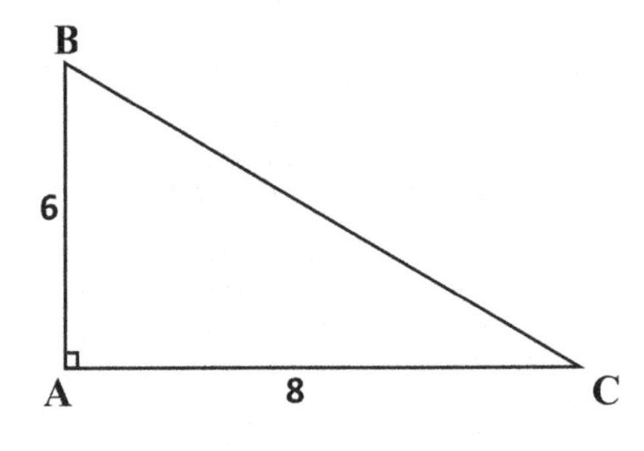

39) The capacity of a red box is 30% bigger than the capacity of a blue box. If the red box can hold 78 equal sized books, how many of the same books can the blue box hold?

A. 25

B. 60

C. 40

D. 50

40) A taxi driver earns $15 per hour work. If he works 6 hours a day, and he uses 3-liters Petrol in 2 hours with price $2.2 for 1-liter. How much money does he earn in one day?

A. $90

B. $82.5

C. $19.8

D. $70.2

Practice Test 6

This is the End of this Section.

Answer Keys

STAAR Practice Tests

❋ Now, it's time to review your results to see where you went wrong and what areas you need to improve!

Practice Test - 1

1	A	**16**	B	**31**	C
2	B	**17**	B	**32**	C
3	A	**18**	A	**33**	D
4	74.8	**19**	168	**34**	B
5	B	**20**	D	**35**	C
6	D	**21**	C	**36**	C
7	B	**22**	C	**37**	D
8	C	**23**	B	**38**	A
9	B	**24**	B	**39**	B
10	B	**25**	D	**40**	A
11	C	**26**	D		
12	D	**27**	D		
13	D	**28**	C		
14	70	**29**	B		
15	B	**30**	A		

Practice Test - 2

1	A	**16**	D	**31**	B
2	B	**17**	B	**32**	B
3	C	**18**	B	**33**	5
4	C	**19**	D	**34**	A
5	B	**20**	B	**35**	C
6	D	**21**	C	**36**	B
7	C	**22**	D	**37**	D
8	210	**23**	D	**38**	C
9	B	**24**	A	**39**	B
10	B	**25**	C	**40**	A
11	A	**26**	B		
12	A	**27**	B		
13	D	**28**	C		
14	D	**29**	C		
15	A	**30**	32		

Practice Test - 3

1	A	**16**	B	**31**	C
2	C	**17**	A	**32**	A
3	A	**18**	B	**33**	A
4	66	**19**	156	**34**	D
5	C	**20**	A	**35**	A
6	A	**21**	C	**36**	C
7	A	**22**	B	**37**	C
8	C	**23**	B	**38**	D
9	C	**24**	C	**39**	A
10	B	**25**	A	**40**	B
11	C	**26**	C		
12	B	**27**	B		
13	D	**28**	C		
14	60	**29**	D		
15	A	**30**	C		

Practice Test - 4

1	D	**16**	D	**31**	A
2	A	**17**	A	**32**	C
3	D	**18**	A	**33**	4
4	B	**19**	C	**34**	C
5	C	**20**	A	**35**	C
6	A	**21**	A	**36**	B
7	D	**22**	D	**37**	A
8	160	**23**	B	**38**	C
9	B	**24**	B	**39**	C
10	A	**25**	A	**40**	D
11	B	**26**	C		
12	A	**27**	B		
13	A	**28**	C		
14	C	**29**	D		
15	B	**30**	72		

Practice Test - 5					
1	A	**16**	B	**31**	C
2	C	**17**	A	**32**	A
3	A	**18**	B	**33**	A
4	69.6	**19**	126	**34**	D
5	C	**20**	A	**35**	A
6	A	**21**	C	**36**	C
7	A	**22**	B	**37**	C
8	C	**23**	B	**38**	D
9	C	**24**	C	**39**	A
10	B	**25**	A	**40**	B
11	C	**26**	C		
12	B	**27**	B		
13	D	**28**	C		
14	50	**29**	D		
15	A	**30**	C		

Practice Test - 6					
1	D	**16**	D	**31**	A
2	A	**17**	A	**32**	C
3	D	**18**	A	**33**	3
4	B	**19**	C	**34**	C
5	C	**20**	A	**35**	C
6	A	**21**	A	**36**	B
7	D	**22**	D	**37**	A
8	130	**23**	D	**38**	C
9	B	**24**	B	**39**	C
10	A	**25**	A	**40**	D
11	B	**26**	C		
12	A	**27**	B		
13	A	**28**	C		
14	C	**29**	D		
15	B	**30**	98		

Answers and Explanations

Practice Test 1

STAAR - Mathematics

Answers and Explanations

1) Answer: A

Use the formula for area of circles.

Area = $\pi r^2 \Rightarrow 49\pi = \pi r^2 \Rightarrow 49 = r^2 \Rightarrow r = 7$

Radius of the circle is 7. Now, use the circumference formula:

Circumference = $2\pi r = 2\pi\,(7) = 14\,\pi$

2) Answer: B

Let x be the number of cans. Write the proportion and solve for x.

$\frac{12 \text{ cans}}{\$\,5.40} = \frac{42 \text{ cans}}{x} \Rightarrow x = \frac{5.40 \times 42}{12} \Rightarrow x = \$18.90$

3) Answer: A

$7x - 5 > 17x - 8.5 - 6.5x$ → Combine like terms:

$7x - 5 > 10.5x - 8.5$ → Subtract $7x$ from both sides: $-5 > 3.5x - 8.5$

Add 8.5 both sides of the inequality.

$3.5 > 3.5x$, Divide both sides by 3.5. ⇒ $\frac{3.5}{3.5} > x \rightarrow x < 1$

4) Answer: 74.8 feet.

Area of a square: $S = a^2 \Rightarrow 349.69 = a^2 \Rightarrow a = 18.7$

Perimeter of a square: $P = 4a \Rightarrow P = 4 \times 18.7 \Rightarrow P = 74.8$

5) Answer: B

Write the proportion and solve for the missing number.

$\frac{12}{39} = \frac{5}{x} \rightarrow 12x = 5 \times 39 = 195$

$12x = 195 \rightarrow x = \frac{195}{12} = 16.25$

6) Answer: D

Let x be the original price.

If the price of a laptop is decreased by 15% to \$425, then:

$85\ \%\ of\ x = 425 \Rightarrow 0.85x = 425 \Rightarrow x = 425 \div 0.85 = 500$

7) Answer: B

let x be the number of gallons of water the container holds when it is full.

Then; $\frac{9}{34}x = 4.5 \rightarrow x = \frac{34 \times 4.5}{9} = 17$

8) Answer: C

$(4^a)^b = 256 \rightarrow 4^{ab} = 256$

$256 = 4^4 \rightarrow 4^{ab} = 4^4 \rightarrow ab = 4$

9) Answer: B

If 20 balls are removed from the bag at random, there will be two ball in the bag.

The probability of choosing a white ball is 2 out of 20. Therefore, the probability of not choosing a white ball is 18 out of 20 and the probability of having not a white ball after removing 18 balls is the same.

10) Answer: B

The value of y in the x-intercept of a line is zero. Then:

$y = 0 \rightarrow -3x + 5(0) = -21 \rightarrow -3x = -21 \rightarrow x = \frac{-21}{-3} = 7$

then, x-intercept of the line is 7

11) Answer: C

Use distributive property:

$3\text{xy}(x - \text{y}) = 3xy(x) + 3xy(-y) = 3yx^2 - 3xy^2$

12) Answer: D

$150 \times \frac{34}{100} = 51.$

13) Answer: D

$y = -2x + 1$

$(-1, 3) \Rightarrow\ 3 = -2(-1) + 1 \Rightarrow 3 = 3$

$(0, 1) \Rightarrow\ 1 = -2(0) + 1 \Rightarrow 1 = 1$

$(3, -5) \Rightarrow\ -5 = -2(3) + 1 \Rightarrow -5 = -5$

$(1, -2) \Rightarrow\ -2 = -2(1) + 1 \Rightarrow -2 \neq -1$

14) Answer: 70.

The perimeter of the trapezoid is 36 cm.

Therefore, the missing side (height) is = 36 – 8 – 12 – 6 = 10

Area of a trapezoid: $A = \frac{1}{2} h (b_1 + b_2) = \frac{1}{2} (10)(6 + 8) = 70$

15) Answer: B

A graph represents y as a function of x if

$x_1 = x_2 \rightarrow y_1 = y_2$

In choice C, for each x, we have two different values for y.

16) Answer: B

$-23 < -5x + 2 < 2 \rightarrow$ Subtract 2 to all sides.

$-23 - 2 < -5x + 2 - 2 < 2 - 2$

$\rightarrow -25 < -5x < 0 \rightarrow$ Divide all sides by -5. (Remember that when you divide all sides of an inequality by a negative number, the inequality sing will be swapped. $<$ becomes $>$)

$\frac{-25}{-5} < \frac{-5x}{-5} < \frac{0}{-5} \Rightarrow 5 > x > 0$, or $0 < x < 5$

17) Answer: B

Use simple interest formula: $I = prt$(I = interest, p = principal, r = rate, t = time)

$I = (16000)(0.0205)(5) = 1{,}640$

18) Answer: A

Compare each mark:

In Algebra Joe scored 22 out of 25 in Algebra. It means Joe scored 88% of the total mark.

$\frac{22}{25} = \frac{x}{100} \Rightarrow x = 88\%$

Joe scored 42 out of 50 in science. It means Joe scored 84% of the total mark. $\frac{42}{50} = \frac{x}{100} \Rightarrow$

$x = 84\%$

Joe scored 17 out of 20 in mathematic that it means 85% of total mark.

$\frac{17}{20} = \frac{x}{100} \Rightarrow x = 85\%$

Therefore, his score in Algebra is higher than his other scores.

19) Answer: 168 m³.

Use the volume of the triangular prism formula.

$V = \frac{1}{2}$ (length) (base) (high)

$V = \frac{1}{2} \times 12 \times 7 \times 4 \Rightarrow V = 168 \text{ m}^3$

20) Answer: D

To find the discount, multiply the number by (100% – rate of discount).

Therefore, for the first discount we get: $(100\% - 15\%)(E) = (0.85)E$

For increase of 6 %:

$(0.85)E \times (100\% + 6\%) = (0.85)(1.06) = 0.901E.$

21) Answer: C

$2x - 6y = -15 \Rightarrow -6y = -2x - 15 \Rightarrow y = \frac{-2}{-6}x - \frac{15}{-6} \Rightarrow y = \frac{1}{3}x + \frac{5}{2}$

$y = \frac{1}{3}x + 2\frac{1}{2}$

22) Answer: C

When a point is reflected over x axes, the (y) coordinate of that point changes to $(-y)$ while its x coordinate remains the same.

C (3, 8) → C' (3, −8)

23) Answer: B

Solving Systems of Equations by Elimination

$\begin{array}{r} 2x + 3y = -2 \\ 5x - y = 12 \end{array}$ Multiply the first equation by 5, and second equation by −2, then add two equations.

$\begin{array}{r} 5(2x + 3y = -2) \\ -2(5x - y = 12) \end{array} \Rightarrow \begin{array}{r} 10x + 15y = -10 \\ -10x + 2y = -24 \end{array} \Rightarrow 17y = -34 \Rightarrow y = -2.$

$5x - y = 12, 5x - (-2) = 12$, then: $x = 2, (2, -2)$

24) Answer: B

To find the discount, multiply the number by (100% – rate of discount).

Therefore, for the first discount we get: (300) (100% – 20%) = (300) (0.8)

For the next 10 % discount: (300) (0.80) (0.90).

25) Answer: D

Use distance formula:

$C = \sqrt{(x_A - x_B)^2 + (y - y_B)^2} \Rightarrow C = \sqrt{(2 - (-1))^2 + (0 - 4)^2}$

$C = \sqrt{(3)^2 + (-4)^2} \Rightarrow C = \sqrt{9 + 16} \Rightarrow C = \sqrt{25} = 5$

26) Answer: D

Percentage of women in city C = $\frac{700}{1365} \times 100 = 51.28\%$

Percentage of men in city B = $\frac{300}{591} \times 100 = 50.76\%$

Percentage of men in city A to percentage of women in city C: $\frac{51.28}{50.76} = 1.01$

27) Answer: D

Ratio of women to men in city A: $\frac{570}{600}$=0.95

Ratio of women to men in city B: $\frac{291}{300}$=0.97

Ratio of women to men in city C: $\frac{665}{700}$=0.95

Ratio of women to men in city D: $\frac{528}{550}$=0.96

28) Answer: C

Solve for each equation: $(3, -4)$

$y = -4 \Rightarrow -4 = -4$

$y = 2x - 10 \Rightarrow -4 = 2(3) - 10 \Rightarrow -4 = -4$

$y = 1 - x \Rightarrow -4 = 1 - 3 \Rightarrow -4 \neq -2$

$y = -x - 1 \Rightarrow -4 = -1 - 3 \Rightarrow -4 = -4$

29) Answer: B

$a + b + c = 62 \Rightarrow \frac{a+b+c+d}{4} = 24 \Rightarrow a + b + c + d = 96$

$\Rightarrow 62 + d = 96 \Rightarrow d = 96 - 62 = 34$

30) Answer: A

39×\$278=\$10,842 Payable amount is: \$13,202 – \$10,842 = \$2,360

31) Answer: C

If two lines are parallel with each other, then the slope of the two lines is the same.

Then in line $y = 3x - 2$, the slope is equal to 3

And in the line $3x - y = -4 \Rightarrow y = 3x + 4$, the slope equal to 3

32) Answer: C

Let x be the smallest number. Then, these are the numbers:

$x, x + 1, x + 2, x + 3$

average $= \frac{\text{sum of terms}}{\text{number of terms}} \Rightarrow 28.5 = \frac{x+(x+1)+(x+2)+(x+3)}{4} \Rightarrow 28.5 = \frac{4x+6}{4}$

$\Rightarrow 114 = 4x + 6 \Rightarrow 108 = 4x \Rightarrow x = 27$

33) Answer: D

Let x be the original price.

If the price of a laptop is decreased by 15% to \$425, then:

$85\ \%\ of\ x = 425 \Rightarrow 0.85x = 425 \Rightarrow x = 425 \div 0.85 = 500$

34) Answer: C

The sum of the weight of all girls is: $16 \times 37 = 592$ kg

The sum of the weight of all boys is: $24 \times 42 = 1008$ kg

The sum of the weight of all students is: $592 + 1008 = 1600$ kg

average $= \frac{\text{sum of terms}}{\text{number of terms}}$; average $= \frac{1600}{40} = 40$

35) Answer: C

$\frac{a + b}{2} = 90 \Rightarrow a + b = 180$

$\frac{a + b + c}{3} = 92 \Rightarrow a + b + c = 276$

$180 + c = 276 \Rightarrow c = 276 - 180 = 96$

36) Answer: C

$x - y = 4$ has a graph that is a straight line. All other options are not equations of straight lines.

37) Answer: D

The sum of supplement angles is 180. Let x be that angle. Therefore,

$x + 8x = 180; 9x = 180$, divide both sides by 9: $x = 20$

38) Answer: A

Let x be the number. Write the equation and solve for x.

$\frac{3}{4} \times 32 = \frac{4}{5} \cdot x \Rightarrow \frac{3\times32}{4} = \frac{4x}{5}$, use cross multiplication to solve for x.

$5 \times 96 = 4x \times 4 \Rightarrow 480 = 16x \Rightarrow x = 30$

39) Answer: B

The probability of choosing a Diamonds is $\frac{13}{52} = \frac{1}{4}$

40) Answer: A

If the score of Harper was 84, therefore the score of Emma is 42. Since, the score of Zoe was one third of Emma, therefore, the score of Zoe is 14.

Practice Test 2

STAAR - Mathematics

Answers and Explanations

1) Answer: A

Use Pythagorean Theorem: $a^2 + b^2 = c^2$

$24^2 + 18^2 = C^2 \Rightarrow 576 + 324 = C^2 \Rightarrow 900 = c^2 \Rightarrow c = 30$

2) Answer: B

Let x be the number. Write the equation and solve for x.

$\frac{(35-x)}{x} = 4$ (cross multiply)

$(35 - x) = 4x$, then add x both sides. $35 = 5x$, now divide both sides by 5. $\Rightarrow x = 7$.

3) Answer: C

Use simple interest formula: $I = prt$;

$(I = interest, p = principal, r = rate, t = time)$

$I = (6{,}000)(0.0225)(4) = 540$

4) Answer: C

Let x be the number of soft drinks for 117 guests. Write the proportion and solve for x.

$\frac{15 \text{ soft drinks}}{9 \text{ guests}} = \frac{x}{117 \text{ guests}} \Rightarrow x = \frac{117 \times 15}{9} \Rightarrow x = 195$

5) Answer: B

6% of the volume of the solution is alcohol. Let x be the volume of the solution. Then:

6% of x = 14.4 ml

$0.06\,x = 14.4 \Rightarrow \frac{6x}{100} = \frac{144}{10}$ cross multiply; $60x = 14400 \Rightarrow$ (devide by 60) $x = 240$

6) Answer: D

Use the area of rectangle formula ($S = a \times b$).

To find area of the shaded region subtract smaller rectangle from bigger rectangle.

$S_1 - S_2 = (7\,ft \times 15ft) - (4ft \times 9ft) \Rightarrow S_1 - S_2 = 69ft.$

7) Answer: C

The weight of 13.4 meters of this rope is: $13.4 \times 450g = 6030g$

1 kg = 1,000 g, therefore, $6{,}030\ g \div 1000 = 6.03kg$

8) Answer: 210

Th ratio of boy to girls is 3:4. Therefore, there are 3 boys out of 7 students. To find the answer, first divide the total number of students by 7, then multiply the result by 3.

$490 \div 7 = 70 \Rightarrow 70 \times 3 = 210$

9) Answer: B

the population is increased by 8% and 15%. 8% increase changes the population to 105% of original population.

For the second increase, multiply the result by 115%.

$(1.08) \times (1.15) = 1.242 = 124.2\%$

24.2 percent of the population is increased after two years.

10)Answer: B

A linear equation is a relationship between two variables, x and y, that can be put in the form $y = mx + b$.

A non-proportional linear relationship takes on the form $y = mx + b$, where $b \neq 0$ and its graph is a line that does not cross through the origin.

11)Answer: A

Four years ago, Amy was four times as old as Mike. Mike is 9 years now. Therefore, 4 years ago Mike was 5 years.

Four years ago, Amy was: $A = 4 \times 5 = 20$

Now Amy is 24 years old: 20 + 4 = 24

12)Answer: A

$|-21+7| - |7(-3)| = |-14| - |-21| = 14 - 21 = -7$

13)Answer: D

$\begin{cases} \frac{-x}{3} + \frac{y}{6} = 2 \\ \frac{-2y}{5} + 2x = -6 \end{cases}$ → Multiply the top equation by 6. Then,

$\begin{cases} -2x + y = 12 \\ \frac{-2y}{5} + 2x = -6 \end{cases}$ → Add two equations.

$\frac{3}{5}y = 6 \rightarrow y = 10$, plug in the value of y into the first equation→ $x = -1$

14) Answer: D

$\frac{5}{7} \times 28 = \frac{140}{7} = 20$

15) Answer: A

Two triangles ΔABC and ΔCD are similar. Then:

$\frac{AB}{DF} = \frac{BC}{CD} \rightarrow \frac{6}{8} = \frac{x}{35 - x} \rightarrow 210 - 6x = 8x \rightarrow 14x = 210 \rightarrow x = 15$

16) Answer: D

The slop of line A is: $m = \frac{y_2 - y_1}{x_2 - x_1} = \frac{4-1}{-1-(-2)} = 3$

Parallel lines have the same slope and only choice D $(2y - 6x = 5 \Rightarrow y = 3x + \frac{5}{2})$ has slope of 3.

17) Answer: B

The perimeter of the rectangle is: $2x + 2y = 28$

$\rightarrow x + y = 14 \rightarrow x = 14 - y$

The area of the rectangle is: $x \times y = 40 \rightarrow (14 - y)(y) = 40$

$\rightarrow y^2 - 14y + 40 = 0$

Solve the quadratic equation by factoring method.

$(y - 4)(y - 10) = 0 \rightarrow y = 4$ (Unacceptable, because y must be greater than 4) or $y = 10$; If $y = 10 \rightarrow x = 14 - y \rightarrow x = 14 - 10 \rightarrow x = 4$

18) Answer: B

Let x be the number of new shoes the team can purchase. Therefore, the team can purchase 125 x.

The team had \$25,000 and spent \$17,000. Now the team can spend on new shoes \$8,000 at most.

Now, write the inequality: $125x + 17{,}000 \leq 25{,}000$

19) Answer: D

Use the formula for Percent of Change

$\frac{\text{New Value} - \text{Old Value}}{\text{Old Value}} \times 100\ \% \Rightarrow \frac{39-60}{60} \times 100\ \% = -35\ \%$

(negative sign here means that the new price is less than old price).

20) Answer: B

Use simple interest formula: $I = prt$ (I = interest, p = principal, r = rate, t = time)

$I = (8000)(0.025)(5) = 1000$

21) Answer: C

Use this formula: Percent of Change = $\frac{\text{New Value} - \text{Old Value}}{\text{Old Value}} \times 100\ \%$

$\frac{18000-24000}{24000} \times 100\ \% = -25\ \%$ and $\frac{13500-18000}{18000} \times 100\% = -25\ \%$

22) Answer: D

The amount of money for x bookshelf is: $50x$

Then, the total cost of all bookshelves is equal to: $50x + 480$

The total cost, in dollar, per bookshelf is: $\frac{\text{Total cost}}{\text{number of items}} = \frac{50x+480}{x}$

23) Answer: D

A. $f(x) = 2x^2 + 2$ if $x = 4 \rightarrow f(4) = 2(4)^2 + 2 = 34 \neq 6$

B. $f(x) = x^2 + 3$ if $x = 4 \rightarrow f(4) = (4)^2 + 3 = 19 \neq 6$

C. $f(x) = \sqrt{2x + 2}$ if $x = 4 \rightarrow f(4) = \sqrt{2(4) + 2} = \sqrt{10} \neq 6$

D. $f(x) = 2\sqrt{x} + 2$ if $x = 4 \rightarrow f(4) = 2\sqrt{4} + 2 = 6$

24) Answer: A

Let x be all expenses, then $\frac{21}{100}x = \$840 \rightarrow x = \frac{100 \times \$840}{21} = \$4{,}000$

He spent for his rent: $\frac{28}{100} \times \$4{,}000 = \$1{,}120$

25) Answer: C

The smallest number is -12. To find the largest possible value of one of the other five integers, we need to choose the smallest possible integers for four of them. Let x be the largest number. Then:

$-50 = (-12) + (-11) + (-10) + (-9) + x \rightarrow -50 = -42 + x$

$\rightarrow x = -50 + 53 = -8$

26) Answer: B

The angles on a straight line add up to 180 degrees. Then: $x + 16 + y + y + 2x = 180$

Then, $3x + 2y = 180 - 16 \rightarrow 3(32) + 2y = 164$

$\rightarrow 2y = 164 - 96 = 68 \rightarrow y = 34$

27) Answer: B

Square root of 49 is $\sqrt{49} = 7 = 7$

Square root of 52 is $\sqrt{52} = \sqrt{49 + 3} > \sqrt{49} = 7$

Square root of 64 is $\sqrt{64} = 8 > 7$

Square root of 36 is $\sqrt{36} = 6 < 7$

Since, $\sqrt{52} < \sqrt{64}$, then the answer is B.

28) Answer: C

To find the area of the shaded region subtract smaller circle from bigger circle.

$S_{bigger} - S_{smaller} = \pi (r_{bigger})^2 - \pi (r_{smaller})^2 \Rightarrow S_{bigger} - S_{smaller} = \pi (7)^2 - \pi (5)^2$

$\Rightarrow 49\pi - 25\pi = 24\pi$

29) Answer: C

$\sqrt{x} = -2 \rightarrow x = 4$

then; $\sqrt{x} - 3 = \sqrt{4} - 3 = 2 - 3 = -1$ and $\sqrt{x + 5} = \sqrt{4 + 5} = \sqrt{9} = 3$

Then: $(\sqrt{x + 5}) + (\sqrt{x} - 3) = 3 + (-1) = 2$

30) Answer: 32.

$a = 8 \Rightarrow$ area of the triangle is

$= \frac{1}{2}(8 \times 8) = \frac{64}{2} = 32\ cm^2$

Isosceles right triangle

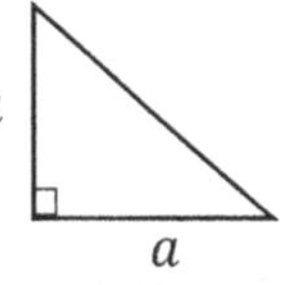

31) Answer: B

x is directly proportional to the square of y. Then: $x = cy^2$

$36 = c(3)^2 \rightarrow 36 = 9c \rightarrow c = \frac{36}{9} = 4$

The relationship between x and y is: $x = 4y^2$, $x = 144$

$144 = 4y^2 \rightarrow y^2 = \frac{144}{4} = 36 \rightarrow y = 6$

32) Answer: B

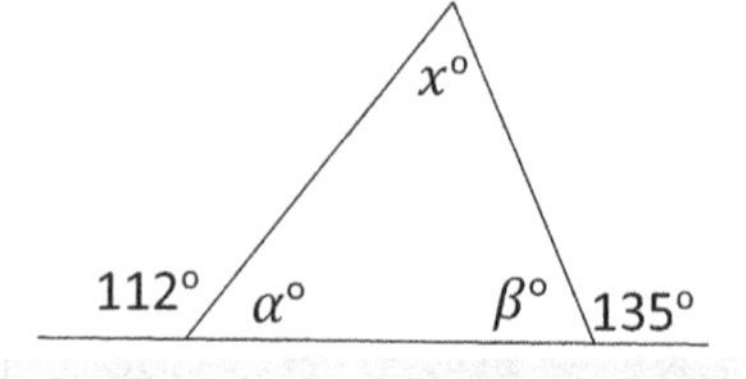

$\alpha = 180° - 112° = 68°$

$\beta = 180° - 135° = 45°$

$x + \alpha + \beta = 180° \rightarrow x = 180° - 68° - 45° = 67°$

33) Answer: 5

Use formula of rectangle prism volume.

V = (length) (width) (height) ⇒ 1800 = (24) (15) (height) ⇒

height = 1800 ÷ 360 = 5

34) Answer: A

The amount of money that jack earns for one hour: $\frac{\$500}{40} = \$12.5$

Number of additional hours that he works to make enough money is: $\frac{\$710-\$500}{1.4\times\$12.5} = 12$

Number of total hours is: $40 + 12 = 52$

35) Answer: C

Let's find the mean (average), mode and median of the number of cities for each type of pollution.

Number of cities for each type of pollution: 6, 3, 4, 9, 8

average (mean) = $\frac{sum\ of\ terms}{number\ of\ terms} = \frac{6+3+4+9+8}{5} = \frac{30}{5} = 6$

Median is the number in the middle. To find median, first list numbers in order from smallest to largest: 3, 4, 6, 8, 9

Median of the data is 6.

Mode is the number which appears most often in a set of numbers. Therefore, there is no mode in the set of numbers.

Median = Mean, then, $a=c$

36) Answer: B

Let the number of cities should be added to type of pollutions C be x. Then:

$\frac{x+3}{8} = 0.750 \rightarrow x+3 = 8 \times 0.750 \rightarrow x+3 = 6 \rightarrow x = 3$

37) Answer: D

Percent of cities in the type of pollution B: $\frac{4}{10} \times 100 = 40\%$

Percent of cities in the type of pollution C: $\frac{3}{10} \times 100 = 30\%$

Percent of cities in the type of pollution E: $\frac{6}{10} \times 100 = 60\%$

38) Answer: C

$AB = 6$, And $AC = 8$

$BC = \sqrt{6^2 + 8^2} = \sqrt{36 + 64} = \sqrt{100} = 10$

Perimeter $= 6 + 8 + 10 = 24$; Area $= \frac{6 \times 8}{2} = 24$

In this case, the ratio of the perimeter of the triangle to its area is: $\frac{24}{24} = 1$

If the sides AB and AC become triple longer, then: $AB = 18$, And $AC = 24$

$BC = \sqrt{18^2 + 24^2} = \sqrt{324 + 576} = \sqrt{900} = 30$

Perimeter $= 18 + 24 + 30 = 72$; Area $= \frac{18 \times 24}{2} = 9 \times 24 = 216$

In this case the ratio of the perimeter of the triangle to its area is: $\frac{72}{216} = \frac{1}{3}$

39) Answer: B

The capacity of a red box is 30% bigger than the capacity of a blue box and it can hold 65 books. Therefore, we want to find a number that 20% bigger than that number is 30. Let x be that number. Then:

$1.30 \times x = 65$, Divide both sides of the equation by 1.3. Then: $x = \frac{65}{1.30} = 50$

40) Answer: A

$\$15 \times 12 = \$180$

Petrol use: $3 \div 2 = 1.5, 12 \times 1.5 = 18$ liters

Petrol cost: $18 \times \$2.50 = \$45$

Money earned: $\$180 - \$45 = \$135$

Practice Test 3

STAAR - Mathematics

Answers and Explanations

1) Answer: A

Use the formula for area of circles.

Area = $\pi r^2 \Rightarrow 36\pi = \pi r^2 \Rightarrow 36 = r^2 \Rightarrow r = 6$

Radius of the circle is 6. Now, use the circumference formula:

Circumference = $2\pi r = 2\pi(6) = 12\pi$

2) Answer: C

Let x be the number of cans. Write the proportion and solve for x.

$\frac{13 \text{ cans}}{\$6{\cdot}40} = \frac{26 \text{ cans}}{x} \Rightarrow x = \frac{6{\cdot}40 \times 26}{13} \Rightarrow x = 12.80$

3) Answer: A

$8x - 5 > 18x - 9.5 - 5.5x \rightarrow$ Combine like terms:

$8x - 5 > 12.5x - 9.5$ Subtract $8x$ from both sides: $-5 > 4.5x - 9.5$

Add 9.5 both sides of the inequality.

$4.5 > 4.5x$, Divide both sides by 4.5. $\Rightarrow \frac{4{\cdot}5}{4{\cdot}5} > x \rightarrow x < 1$

4) Answer: 66 feet.

Area of a square: $S = a^2 \Rightarrow 272.25 = a^2 \Rightarrow a = 16.5$

Perimeter of a square: $P = 4a \Rightarrow P = 4 \times 16.5 \Rightarrow P = 66$

5) Answer: C

Write the proportion and solve for the missing number.

$\frac{14}{42} = \frac{6}{x} \rightarrow 14x = 6 \times 42 = 252 \rightarrow 14x = 252 \rightarrow x = \frac{252}{14} = 18$

6) Answer: A

Let x be the original price.

If the price of a laptop is decreased by 20% to \$345, then:

$80\%\ of\ x = 345 \Rightarrow 0.80x = 345 \Rightarrow x = 345 \div 0.80 = 431.25$

7) Answer: A

let x be the number of gallons of water the container holds when it is full.

Then; $\frac{8}{44}x = 5.6 \rightarrow x = \frac{44 \times 5.6}{8} = 30.8$

8) Answer: C

$(3^a)^b = 729 \rightarrow 3^{ab} = 729 \rightarrow 729 = 3^6 \rightarrow 3^{ab} = 3^6 \rightarrow ab = 6$

9) Answer: C

If 19 balls are removed from the bag at random, there will be three ball in the bag.

The probability of choosing a white ball is 3 out of 19. Therefore, the probability of not choosing a white ball is 16 out of 19 and the probability of having not a white ball after removing 16 balls is the same.

10)Answer: B

The value of y in the x-intercept of a line is zero. Then:

$y = 0 \rightarrow -4x + 7(0) = -24 \rightarrow -4x = -24 \rightarrow x = \frac{-24}{-4} = 6$

then, x-intercept of the line is 6

11)Answer: C

Use distributive property:

$4xy(2x - y) = 4xy(2x) + 4xy(-y) = 8yx^2 - 4xy^2$

12) Answer: B

$120 \times \frac{40}{100} = 48.$

13)Answer: D

$y = -3x + 2$

$(-1, -2) \Rightarrow -2 = -3(-1) - 2 \Rightarrow 1 = -2$

$(1, -1) \Rightarrow -1 = -3(1) + 2 \Rightarrow -1 = -1$

$(3, -7) \Rightarrow -7 = -3(3) + 2 \Rightarrow -7 = -7$

$(1, 1) \Rightarrow 1 = -3(1) + 2 \Rightarrow 1 \neq -1$

14)Answer: 60.

The perimeter of the trapezoid is 32 cm.

Therefore, the missing side (height) is = 32 – 7 – 10 – 5 = 10

Area of a trapezoid: $A = \frac{1}{2} h (b_1 + b_2) = \frac{1}{2} (10) (5 + 7) = 60$

15) Answer: A

A graph represents y as a function of x if $x_1 = x_2 \rightarrow y_1 = y_2$

In choice A, for each x, we have two different values for y.

16) Answer: B

$-21 < -4x + 3 < 3 \rightarrow$ Subtract 3 to all sides.

$-21 - 3 < -4x + 3 - 3 < 3 - 3$

$\rightarrow -24 < -4x < 0 \rightarrow$ Divide all sides by -4. (Remember that when you divide all sides of an inequality by a negative number, the inequality sing will be swapped. < becomes >)

$\frac{-24}{-4} < \frac{-4x}{-4} < \frac{0}{-4} \Rightarrow 6 > x > 0$, or $0 < x < 6$

17) Answer: A

Use simple interest formula: $I = prt$(I = interest, p = principal, r = rate, t = time)

I = (18,000) (0.0175) (4) = 1,260

18) Answer: B

Compare each mark:

In Algebra Joe scored 20 out of 35 in Algebra. It means Joe scored 57% of the total mark.

$\frac{20}{35} = \frac{x}{100} \Rightarrow x = 57\%$

Joe scored 48 out of 55 in science. It means Joe scored 87% of the total mark. $\frac{48}{55} = \frac{x}{100} \Rightarrow$

$x = 87\%$

Joe scored 16 out of 20 in mathematic that it means 80% of total mark.

$\frac{16}{20} = \frac{x}{100} \Rightarrow x = 80\%$

Therefore, his score in Science is higher than his other scores.

19) Answer: 156 m^3.

Use the volume of the triangular prism formula.

$V = \frac{1}{2}$ (length) (base) (high)

$V = \frac{1}{2} \times 13 \times 8 \times 3 \Rightarrow V = 156\ m^3$

20) Answer: A

To find the discount, multiply the number by (100% – rate of discount).

Therefore, for the first discount we get: $(100\% - 20\%)(E) = (0.80)\ E$

For increase of 8 %:

$(0.80)\ E \times (100\% + 8\%) = (0.80)\ (1.08) = 0.864E$

21) Answer: C

$3x - 6y = -18 \Rightarrow -6y = -3x - 18 \Rightarrow y = \frac{-3}{-6}x - \frac{18}{-6} \Rightarrow y = \frac{1}{2}x + 3$

$y = \frac{1}{2}x + 3$

22) Answer: B

When a point is reflected over x axes, the (y) coordinate of that point changes to $(-y)$ while its x coordinate remains the same.

B (2, 6) → B' (2, −6)

23) Answer: B

Solving Systems of Equations by Elimination

$$\begin{array}{l} 2x + y = -5 \\ 3x - 2y = 10 \end{array}$$

Multiply the first equation by 3, and second equation by −2, then add two equations.

$$\begin{array}{r} 3(2x + y = -5) \\ -2(3x - 2y = 10) \end{array} \Rightarrow \begin{array}{r} 6x + 3y = -15 \\ -6x + 4y = -20 \end{array} \Rightarrow 7y = -35 \Rightarrow y = -5.$$

$2x + y = -5,\ 2x + (-5) = -5$, then: $x = 0,\ (0, -5)$

24) Answer: C

To find the discount, multiply the number by (100% – rate of discount).

Therefore, for the first discount we get: (400) (100% – 25%) = (400) (0.75)

For the next 15 % discount: (400) (0.75) (0.85).

25) Answer: A

Use distance formula:

$C = \sqrt{(x_A - x_B)^2 + (y - y_B)^2} \Rightarrow C = \sqrt{(3 - (-1))^2 + (1 - (-2))^2}$

$C = \sqrt{(4)^2 + (3)^2} \Rightarrow C = \sqrt{16 + 9} \Rightarrow C = \sqrt{25} = 5$

26) Answer: C

Percentage of women in city A = $\frac{570}{1,170} \times 100 = 48.71\%$

Percentage of men in city B = $\frac{300}{591} \times 100 = 50.72\%$

Percentage of men in city B to percentage of women in city A: $\frac{48.71}{50.72}$ =0.96

27) Answer: B

Ratio of women to men in city A: $\frac{570}{600}$=0.95

Ratio of women to men in city B: $\frac{291}{300}$=0.97

Ratio of women to men in city C: $\frac{665}{700}$=0.95

Ratio of women to men in city D: $\frac{528}{550}$=0.96

28) Answer: C

Solve for each equation: $(2, -5)$

$y = -5 \Rightarrow -5 = -5$

$y = 3x - 11 \Rightarrow -5 = 3(2) - 11 \Rightarrow -5 = -5$

$y = -1 - x \Rightarrow -5 = -1 - 2 \Rightarrow -5 \neq -3$

$y = -x - 3 \Rightarrow -5 = -2 - 3 \Rightarrow -5 = -5$

29) Answer: D

$a + b + c + d = 84 \Rightarrow \frac{a+b+c+d+e}{5} = 28 \Rightarrow a + b + c + d + e = 140$

$\Rightarrow 84 + e = 140 \Rightarrow e = 140 - 84 = 56$

30) Answer: C

42×\$245=\$10,290 Payable amount is: \$14,101−10,290 = 3,811

31) Answer: C

If two lines are parallel with each other, then the slope of the two lines is the same.

Then in line $y = 2x - 3$, the slope is equal to 2

And in the line $2x - y = -4 \Rightarrow y = 2x + 4$, the slope equal to 2

32) Answer: A

Let x be the smallest number. Then, these are the numbers:

$x, x+1, x+2, x+3, x+4$

average $= \frac{\text{sum of terms}}{\text{number of terms}} \Rightarrow 36 = \frac{x+(x+1)+(x+2)+(x+3)+(x+4)}{5} \Rightarrow 36 = \frac{5x+10}{5}$

$\Rightarrow 180 = 5x + 10 \Rightarrow 170 = 5x \Rightarrow x = 34$

33)Answer: A

Let x be the original price.

If the price of a laptop is decreased by 15% to \$425, then:

$75\ \%\ of\ x = 390 \Rightarrow 0.75\ x = 390 \Rightarrow x = 390 \div 0.75 = 520$

34)Answer: D

The sum of the weight of all girls is: $18 \times 35 = 630$ kg

The sum of the weight of all boys is: $22 \times 45 = 990$ kg

The sum of the weight of all students is: $630 + 990 = 1{,}620$ kg

average $= \frac{\text{sum of terms}}{\text{number of terms}}$; average $= \frac{1{,}620}{40} = 40.50$

35)Answer: A

$\frac{a+b+c}{3} = 80 \Rightarrow a + b + c = 240$

$\frac{a+b+c+d}{4} = 78 \Rightarrow a + b + c + d = 312$

$240 + d = 312 \Rightarrow d = 312 - 240 = 72$

36)Answer: C

$x - y = 6$ has a graph that is a straight line. All other options are not equations of straight lines.

37)Answer: C

The sum of supplement angles is 180. Let x be that angle. Therefore,

$x + 5x = 180$; $6x = 180$, divide both sides by 6: $x = 30$

38)Answer: D

Let x be the number. Write the equation and solve for x.

$\frac{1}{4} \times 36 = \frac{3}{5}\ x \Rightarrow \frac{1 \times 36}{4} = \frac{3x}{5}$, use cross multiplication to solve for x.

$180 = 3x \times 4 \Rightarrow 180 = 12x \Rightarrow x = 15$

39) Answer: A

The probability of choosing a Hearts is $\frac{13}{52} = \frac{1}{4}$

40) Answer: B

If the score of Harper was 90, therefore the score of Emma is 30. Since, the score of Zoe was one third of Emma, therefore, the score of Zoe is 6.

Practice Test 4

STAAR - Mathematics

Answers and Explanations

1) Answer: D

Use Pythagorean Theorem: $a^2 + b^2 = c^2$

$20^2 + 15^2 = C^2 \Rightarrow 400 + 225 = C^2 \Rightarrow 625 = c^2 \Rightarrow c = 25$

2) Answer: A

Let x be the number. Write the equation and solve for x. $\frac{(42-x)}{x} = 6$ (cross multiply)

$(42 - x) = 6x$, then add x both sides. $42 = 7x$, now divide both sides by 7. $\Rightarrow x = 6$.

3) Answer: D

Use simple interest formula: $I = prt$; (I=interest. p=principal. r=rate. t=time)

$I = (8{,}000)\ (0.0125)\ (2) = 200$

4) Answer: B

Let x be the number of soft drinks for 132 guests. Write the proportion and solve for x.

$\frac{14 \text{ soft drinks}}{11 \text{ guests}} = \frac{x}{132 \text{ guests}} \Rightarrow x = \frac{132 \times 14}{11} \Rightarrow x = 168$

5) Answer: C

7% of the volume of the solution is alcohol. Let x be the volume of the solution. Then:

7% of x = 16.1 ml

$0.07\,x = 16.1 \Rightarrow \frac{7x}{100} = \frac{161}{10}$ cross multiply; $70x = 16{,}100 \Rightarrow$ (devide by 70) $x = 230$

6) Answer: A

Use the area of rectangle formula ($S = a \times b$).

To find area of the shaded region subtract smaller rectangle from bigger rectangle.

$S_1 - S_2 = (6\,ft \times 14ft) - (3ft \times 8ft) \Rightarrow S_1 - S_2 = 60ft.$

7) Answer: D

The weight of 15.8 meters of this rope is: $15.8 \times 330g = 5{,}214g$

1 kg = 1,000 g, therefore, $5{,}214\ g \div 1000 = 5.214$kg

8) Answer: 160

The ratio of boy to girls is 2:5. Therefore, there are 2 boys out of 7 students. To find the answer, first divide the total number of students by 7, then multiply the result by 2.

$560 \div 7 = 80 \Rightarrow 80 \times 2 = 160$

9) Answer: B

the population is increased by 7% and 20%. 7% increase changes the population to 107% of original population.

For the second increase, multiply the result by 120%.

$(1.07) \times (1.20) = (1.284) = 128.40\ \%$

28.40 percent of the population is increased after two years.

10) Answer: A

A linear equation is a relationship between two variables, x and y, that can be put in the form $y = mx + b$.

A non-proportional linear relationship takes on the form $y = mx + b$, where $b \neq 0$ and its graph is a line that does not cross through the origin.

11) Answer: B

Five years ago, Amy was five times as old as Mike. Mike is 10 years now. Therefore, 5 years ago Mike was 5 years.

Five years ago, Amy was: $A = 5 \times 5 = 25$

Now Amy is 25 years old: $25 + 5 = 30$

12) Answer: A

$|-20 + 11| - |8\,(-2)| = |-9| - |-16| = 9 - 16 = -7$

13) Answer: A

$\begin{cases} \frac{-x}{3} + \frac{y}{2} = 4 \\ \frac{-2y}{3} + 4x = -16 \end{cases} \rightarrow$ Multiply the top equation by 12. Then,

$\begin{cases} -4x + 6y = 48 \\ \frac{-2y}{3} + 4x = -16 \end{cases} \rightarrow$ Add two equations.

$\frac{16}{3}y = 32 \rightarrow y = 6$, plug in the value of y into the first equation $\rightarrow x = -3$

14) Answer: C

$\frac{3}{8} \times 32 = \frac{96}{8} = 12$

15) Answer: B

Two triangles ΔABC and ΔCD are similar. Then:

$\frac{AB}{DF} = \frac{BC}{CD} \to \frac{5}{7} = \frac{x}{36 - x} \to 180 - 5x = 7x \to 12x = 180 \to x = 15$

16) Answer: D

The slop of line A is: $m = \frac{y_2 - y_1}{x_2 - x_1} = \frac{5-(-3)}{1-(-3)} = 2$

Parallel lines have the same slope and only choice D ($3y - 6x = 5 \Rightarrow y = 2x + \frac{5}{3}$) has slope of 2.

17) Answer: A

The perimeter of the rectangle is: $2x + 2y = 32$

$\to x + y = 16 \to x = 16 - y$

The area of the rectangle is: $x \times y = 48 \to (16 - y)(y) = 48$

$\to y^2 - 16y + 48 = 0$

Solve the quadratic equation by factoring method.

$(y - 4)(y - 12) = 0 \to y = 4$ (Unacceptable, because y must be greater than 6) or $y = 12$; If $y = 12 \to x = 16 - y \to x = 16 - 12 \to x = 4$

18) Answer: A

Let x be the number of new shoes the team can purchase. Therefore, the team can purchase 115 x.

The team had \$30,000 and spent \$19,000. Now the team can spend on new shoes \$11,000 at most.

Now, write the inequality: $115x + 19{,}000 \leq 30{,}000$

19) Answer: C

Use the formula for Percent of Change

$\frac{\text{New Value} - \text{Old Value}}{Old\ Value} \times 100\ \% \Rightarrow \frac{45-90}{90} \times 100\ \% = -50\ \%$

(negative sign here means that the new price is less than old price).

20) Answer: A

Use simple interest formula: $I = prt$ (I = interest, p = principal, r = rate, t = time)

$I = (10.000)(0.015)(4) = 600$

21) Answer: A

Use this formula: Percent of Change $= \frac{\text{New Value} - \text{Old Value}}{Old\ Value} \times 100\ \%$

$\frac{16{,}000 - 20{,}000}{20{,}000} \times 100\ \% = -20\ \%$ and $\frac{12{,}800 - 16{,}000}{16{,}000} \times 100\% = -20\ \%$

22) Answer: D

The amount of money for x bookshelf is: $65x$

Then, the total cost of all bookshelves is equal to: $65x + 540$

The total cost, in dollar, per bookshelf is: $\frac{Total\ cost}{number\ of\ items} = \frac{65x + 540}{x}$

23) Answer: B

A. $f(x) = x^2 + 2$ if $x = 4 \rightarrow f(4) = (4)^2 + 2 = 18 \neq 16$

B. $f(x) = x^2$ if $x = 4 \rightarrow f(4) = (4)^2 = 16 = 16$

C. $f(x) = \sqrt{x + 5}$ if $x = 4 \rightarrow f(4) = \sqrt{(4) + 5} = \sqrt{9} = 3 \neq 16$

D. $f(x) = 2\sqrt{x} + 2$ if $x = 4 \rightarrow f(4) = 2\sqrt{4} + 2 = 6 \neq 16$

24) Answer: B

Let x be all expenses, then $\frac{20}{100}x = \$720 \rightarrow x = \frac{100 \times \$720}{20} = \$3{,}600$

He spent for his rent: $\frac{26}{100} \times \$3{,}600 = \$936$

25) Answer: A

The smallest number is -10. To find the largest possible value of one of the other four integers, we need to choose the smallest possible integers for three of them. Let x be the largest number. Then:

$-34 = (-10) + (-9) + (-8) + x \rightarrow -34 = -27 + x$

$\rightarrow x = -34 + 27 = -7$

26) Answer: C

The angles on a straight line add up to 180 degrees. Then: $x + 14 + y + y + 2x = 180$

Then, $3x + 2y = 180 - 14 \rightarrow 3(28) + y = 166$

$\rightarrow 2y = 166 - 84 = 82 \rightarrow y = 41$

27) Answer: B

Square root of 51 is $\sqrt{51} = \sqrt{36+15} > \sqrt{36} = 6$

Square root of 40 is $\sqrt{40} = \sqrt{36+4} > \sqrt{36} = 6$

Square root of 64 is $\sqrt{64} = 8 > 6$

Square root of 25 is $\sqrt{25} = 5 < 6$

Since, $\sqrt{25} < \sqrt{36}$, then the answer is B.

28) Answer: C

To find the area of the shaded region subtract smaller circle from bigger circle.

$S_{bigger} - S_{smaller} = \pi (r_{bigger})^2 - \pi (r_{smaller})^2 \Rightarrow S_{bigger} - S_{smaller} = \pi (6)^2 - \pi (4)^2$

$\Rightarrow 36\pi - 16\pi = 20\pi$

29) Answer: D

$\sqrt{x} = -3 \rightarrow x = 9$

then; $\sqrt{x} - 2 = \sqrt{9} - 2 = 3 - 2 = 1$ and $\sqrt{x+7} = \sqrt{9+7} = \sqrt{16} = 4$

Then: $(\sqrt{x+7}) + (\sqrt{x} - 2) = 4 + 1 = 5$

30) Answer: 72.

$a = 12 \Rightarrow$ area of the triangle is

$= \frac{1}{2}(12 \times 12) = \frac{144}{2} = 72\ cm^2$

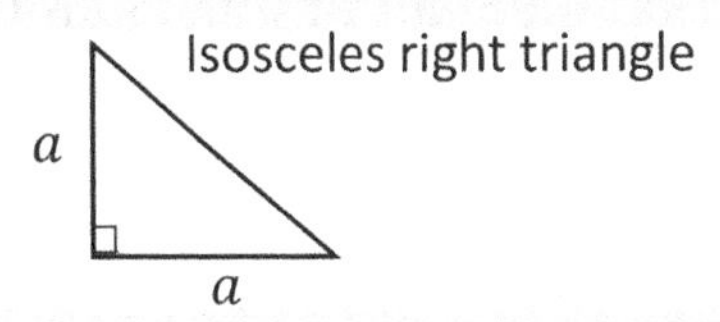

31) Answer: A

x is directly proportional to the square of y. Then: $x = cy^2$

$32 = c(2)^2 \rightarrow 32 = 4c \rightarrow c = \frac{32}{4} = 8$

The relationship between x and y is: $x = 8y^2$, $x = 128$

$128 = 8y^2 \rightarrow y^2 = \frac{128}{8} = 16 \rightarrow y = 4$

32) Answer: C

$\alpha = 180° - 130° = 50°$

$\beta = 180° - 125° = 55°$

$x + \alpha + \beta = 180° \rightarrow x = 180° - 50° - 55° = 75°$

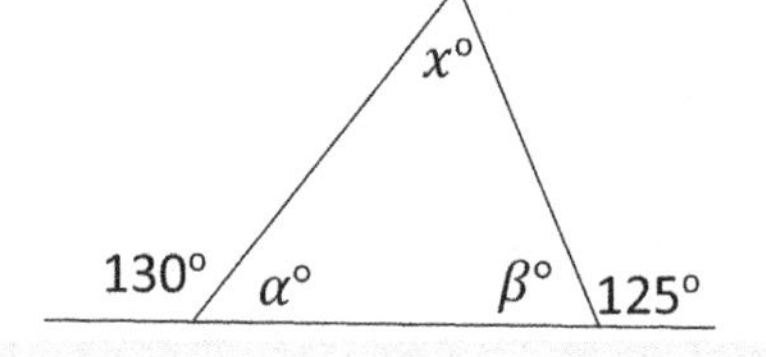

33) Answer: 4

Use formula of rectangle prism volume.

V = (length) (width) (height) ⇒ 1,248 = (26) (12) (height)

⇒ height = 1,248 ÷ 312 = 4

34) Answer: C

The amount of money that jack earns for one hour: $\frac{\$600}{30} = \$20$

Number of additional hours that he works to make enough money is: $\frac{\$1,120-\$600}{2\times\$20} = 13$

Number of total hours is: $30 + 13 = 43$

35) Answer: C

Let's find the mean (average), mode and median of the number of cities for each type of pollution.

Number of cities for each type of pollution: 5, 3, 4, 10, 8

average (mean) = $\frac{sum\ of\ terms}{number\ of\ terms} = \frac{5+3+4+10+8}{5} = \frac{30}{5} = 6$

Median is the number in the middle.

To find median, first list numbers in order from smallest to largest: 3, 4, 5, 8, 10

Median of the data is 5.

Mode is the number which appears most often in a set of numbers. Therefore, there is no mode in the set of numbers.

Median = Mean, then, $c < a$

36) Answer: B

Let the number of cities should be added to type of pollutions B be x. Then:

$\frac{x+4}{10} = 0.80 \rightarrow x + 4 = 10 \times 0.80 \rightarrow x + 4 = 8 \rightarrow x = 4$

37)Answer: A

Percent of cities in the type of pollution A: $\frac{8}{10} \times 100 = 80\%$

Percent of cities in the type of pollution C: $\frac{3}{10} \times 100 = 30\%$

Percent of cities in the type of pollution E: $\frac{5}{10} \times 100 = 50\%$

38)Answer: C

$AB = 9$, And $AC = 12$

$BC = \sqrt{9^2 + 12^2} = \sqrt{81 + 144} = \sqrt{225} = 15$

Perimeter $= 9 + 12 + 15 = 36$; Area $= \frac{9 \times 12}{2} = 54$

In this case, the ratio of the perimeter of the triangle to its area is: $\frac{36}{54} = \frac{4}{5}$

If the sides AB and AC become double longer, then: $AB = 18$, And $AC = 24$

$BC = \sqrt{18^2 + 24^2} = \sqrt{324 + 576} = \sqrt{900} = 30$

Perimeter $= 18 + 24 + 30 = 72$; Area $= \frac{18 \times 24}{2} = 9 \times 24 = 216$

In this case the ratio of the perimeter of the triangle to its area is: $\frac{72}{216} = \frac{1}{3}$

39)Answer: C

The capacity of a red box is 20% bigger than the capacity of a blue box and it can hold 84 books. Therefore, we want to find a number that 20% bigger than that number is 84. Let x be that number. Then:

$1.20 \times x = 84$, Divide both sides of the equation by 1.2. Then: $x = \frac{84}{1.20} = 70$

40)Answer: D

$\$14 \times 8 = \$112$

Petrol use: $4 \div 2 = 2 . 8 \times 2 = 16$ liters

Petrol cost: $16 \times \$1.75 = \$28$

Money earned: $\$112 - \$28 = \$84$

Practice Test 5

STAAR - Mathematics

Answers and Explanations

1) Answer: A

Use the formula for area of circles.

Area = $\pi r^2 \Rightarrow 49\pi = \pi r^2 \Rightarrow 49 = r^2 \Rightarrow r = 7$

Radius of the circle is 7. Now, use the circumference formula:

Circumference = $2\pi r = 2\pi\ (7) = 14\pi$

2) Answer: C

Let x be the number of cans. Write the proportion and solve for x.

$\frac{14 \text{ cans}}{\$\,3.80} = \frac{52 \text{ cans}}{x} \Rightarrow x = \frac{3.80 \times 52}{14} \Rightarrow x = \$14.11$

3) Answer: A

$-9x + 25.5 > -12x + 14.5 + 8.5x \rightarrow$ Combine like terms:

$-9x + 25.5 > -3.5x + 14.5$ Subtract $9x$ from both sides: $25.5 > 5.5x + 14.5$

Add -14.5 both sides of the inequality.

$11 > 5.5x$, Divide both sides by 5.5. $\Rightarrow \frac{11}{5.5} > x \rightarrow x < 2$

4) Answer: 69.6 feet.

Area of a square: $S = a^2 \Rightarrow 302.76 = a^2 \Rightarrow a = 17.4$

Perimeter of a square: $P = 4a \Rightarrow P = 4 \times 17.4 \Rightarrow P = 69.6$

5) Answer: C

Write the proportion and solve for the missing number.

$\frac{16}{34} = \frac{8}{x} \rightarrow 16x = 8 \times 34 = 272 \rightarrow 16x = 272 \rightarrow x = \frac{272}{16} = 17$

6) Answer: A

Let x be the original price.

If the price of a laptop is decreased by 35% to \$580, then:

$65\ \%\ of x = 580 \Rightarrow 0.65x = 580 \Rightarrow x = 580 \div 0.65 = 892.30$

7) Answer: A

let x be the number of gallons of water the container holds when it is full.

Then; $\frac{8}{41}x = 4.8 \rightarrow x = \frac{41 \times 4.8}{8} = 24.6$

8) Answer: C

$(4^a)^b = 256 \rightarrow 4^{ab} = 256 \rightarrow 256 = 4^4 \rightarrow 4^{ab} = 4^4 \rightarrow ab = 4$

9) Answer: C

If 18 balls are removed from the bag at random, there will be one ball in the bag.

The probability of choosing a white ball is 1 out of 20. Therefore, the probability of not choosing a white ball is 18 out of 20 and the probability of having not a white ball after removing 18 balls is the same.

10)Answer: B

The value of y in the x-intercept of a line is zero. Then:

$y = 0 \rightarrow -9x + 5(0) = 63 \rightarrow -9x = 63 \rightarrow x = \frac{-63}{9} = -7$

then, x-intercept of the line is -7

11)Answer: C

Use distributive property:

$8x^3y(3x + 2y) = 8x^3y(3x) + 8x^3y(2y) = 24yx^4 + 16x^3y^2$

12) Answer: B

$150 \times \frac{30}{100} = 45.$

13)Answer: D

$y = -2x + 5$

$(4, -3) \Rightarrow -3 = -2(4) + 5 \Rightarrow -3 = -3$

$(1, 3) \Rightarrow 3 = -2(1) + 5 \Rightarrow 3 = 3$

$(-1, 7) \Rightarrow 7 = -2(-1) + 5 \Rightarrow 7 = 7$

$(1, -1) \Rightarrow -1 = -2(1) + 5 \Rightarrow -1 \neq 3$

14)Answer: 50.

The perimeter of the trapezoid is 28 cm.

Therefore, the missing side (height) is = 28 – 8 – 6 – 4 = 10

Area of a trapezoid: $A = \frac{1}{2} h (b_1 + b_2) = \frac{1}{2} (10)(4 + 6) = 50$

15) Answer: A

A graph represents y as a function of x if $x_1 = x_2 \rightarrow y_1 = y_2$

In choice A, for each x, we have two different values for y.

16) Answer: B

$-43 < -7x + 6 < 6 \rightarrow$ Subtract 6 to all sides.

$-43 - 6 < -7x + 6 - 6 < 6 - 6$

$\rightarrow -49 < -7x < 0 \rightarrow$ Divide all sides by -7. (Remember that when you divide all sides of an inequality by a negative number, the inequality sing will be swapped. $<$ becomes $>$)

$\frac{-49}{-7} < \frac{-7x}{-7} < \frac{0}{-7} \Rightarrow 7 > x > 0$, or $0 < x < 7$

17) Answer: A

Use simple interest formula: $I = prt$ (I = interest, p = principal, r = rate, t = time)

$I = (22{,}000)(0.0225)(5) = 2{,}475$

18) Answer: B

Compare each mark:

In Algebra Joe scored 34 out of 48 in Algebra. It means Joe scored 70.83% of the total mark. $\frac{34}{48} = \frac{x}{100} \Rightarrow x = 70.83\%$

Joe scored 26 out of 32 in science. It means Joe scored 81.25% of the total mark. $\frac{26}{32} = \frac{x}{100}$ $\Rightarrow x = 81.25\%$

Joe scored 15 out of 22 in mathematic that it means 68.18% of total mark.

$\frac{15}{22} = \frac{x}{100} \Rightarrow x = 68.18\%$

Therefore, his score in Science is higher than his other scores.

19) Answer: 126 m^3.

Use the volume of the triangular prism formula.

$V = \frac{1}{2}$ (length) (base) (high)

$V = \frac{1}{2} \times 9 \times 7 \times 4 \Rightarrow V = 126\ m^3$

20) Answer: A

To find the discount, multiply the number by (100% – rate of discount).

Therefore, for the first discount we get: $(100\% - 22\%)(E)$ = (0.78) E

For increase of 5 %:

(0.78) $E \times (100\% + 5\%)$ = (0.78) (1.05) = 0.819E

21) Answer: C

$2x - 4y = 16 \Rightarrow -4y = -2x + 16 \Rightarrow y = \frac{-2}{-4}x + \frac{16}{-4} \Rightarrow y = \frac{1}{2}x - 4$

$y = \frac{1}{2}x - 4$

22) Answer: B

When a point is reflected over x axes, the (y) coordinate of that point changes to $(-y)$ while its x coordinate remains the same.

B (1, 8) → B' (1, −8)

23) Answer: B

Solving Systems of Equations by Elimination

$\begin{array}{l} 5x - 4y = 13 \\ \underline{2x + 3y = \ -4} \end{array}$ Multiply the first equation by -2, and second equation by 5, then add two equations.

$\begin{array}{l} -2(5x - 4y = 13) \\ \underline{5(2x + 3y = -4)} \end{array} \Rightarrow \begin{array}{l} -10x + 8y = -26 \\ 10x + 15y = -20 \end{array} \Rightarrow 23y = -46 \Rightarrow y = -2.$

$2x + 3y = -4$, $2x + 3(-2) = -4$, then: $x = 1$, $(1, -2)$

24) Answer: C

To find the discount, multiply the number by (100% – rate of discount).

Therefore, for the first discount we get: (700) (100% – 30%) = (400) (0.70)

For the next 12 % discount: (700) (0.70) (0.88).

25) Answer: A

Use distance formula:

$C = \sqrt{(x_A - x_B)^2 + (y - y_B)^2} \Rightarrow C = \sqrt{(4 - (-8))^2 + (2 - (-3))^2}$

$C = \sqrt{(12)^2 + (5)^2} \Rightarrow C = \sqrt{144 + 25} \Rightarrow C = \sqrt{169} = 13$

26) Answer: C

Percentage of women in city C = $\frac{740}{1,390} \times 100 = 53.23\%$

Percentage of men in city B = $\frac{280}{620} \times 100 = 45.16\%$

Percentage of women in city C to percentage of men in city B: $\frac{53.23}{45.16} = 1.18$

27) Answer: B

Ratio of women to men in city A: $\frac{520}{680}$=0.76

Ratio of women to men in city B: $\frac{280}{340}$=0.82

Ratio of women to men in city C: $\frac{650}{740}$=0.87

Ratio of women to men in city D: $\frac{520}{570}$=0.91

28) Answer: C

Solve for each equation: $(4, \; -7)$

$y = -7 \Rightarrow -7 = -7$

$y = -2x + 1 \Rightarrow -7 = -2(4) + 1 \Rightarrow -7 = -7$

$y = -2 + x \Rightarrow -7 = -2 + 4 \Rightarrow 2 \neq -3$

$y = -3x + 5 \Rightarrow -7 = -3(4) + 5 \Rightarrow -7 = -7$

29) Answer: D

$a + b + c + d + e = 98 \Rightarrow \frac{a+b+c+d+e+f}{6} = 32 \Rightarrow \mathrm{a} + \mathrm{b} + \mathrm{c} + d + e + f = 192$

$\Rightarrow 98 + f = 192 \Rightarrow f = 192 - 98 = 94$

30) Answer: C

38×\$324=\$12,312 Payable amount is: \$15,435−12,312 = 3,123

31) Answer: C

If two lines are parallel with each other, then the slope of the two lines is the same.

Then in line $y = 8x - 5$, the slope is equal to 8

And in the line $8x - y = -11 \Rightarrow y = 8x + 11$, the slope equal to 8

32) Answer: A

Let x be the smallest number. Then, these are the numbers:

$x, x+1, x+2, x+3, x+4, x+5$

average $= \frac{\text{sum of terms}}{\text{number of terms}} \Rightarrow 22.5 = \frac{x+(x+1)+(x+2)+(x+3)+(x+4)+(x+5)}{6} \Rightarrow 22.5 = \frac{6x+15}{6}$

$\Rightarrow 135 = 6x + 15 \Rightarrow 120 = 6x \Rightarrow x = 20$

33) Answer: A

Let x be the original price.

If the price of a laptop is decreased by 16% to \$378, then:

$84\ \%\ of\ x = 378 \Rightarrow 0.84\ x = 378 \Rightarrow x = 378 \div 0.84 = 450$

34) Answer: D

The sum of the weight of all girls is: $16 \times 40 = 640$ kg

The sum of the weight of all boys is: $29 \times 50 = 1{,}450$ kg

The sum of the weight of all students is: $640 + 1{,}450 = 2{,}090$ kg

average $= \frac{\text{sum of terms}}{\text{number of terms}}$; average $= \frac{2{,}090}{45} = 46.44$

35) Answer: A

$\frac{a+b+c+d}{4} = 76 \Rightarrow a + b + c + d = 304$

$\frac{a+b+c+d+e}{5} = 72 \Rightarrow a + b + c + d + e = 360$

$304 + e = 360 \Rightarrow e = 360 - 304 = 56$

36) Answer: C

$x - y = 8$ has a graph that is a straight line. All other options are not equations of straight lines.

37) Answer: C

The sum of supplement angles is 180. Let x be that angle. Therefore,

$x + 7x = 180$; $8x = 180$, divide both sides by 8: $x = 22.5$

38) Answer: D

Let x be the number. Write the equation and solve for x.

$\frac{2}{9} \times 27 = \frac{6}{11} x \Rightarrow \frac{2 \times 27}{9} = \frac{6x}{11}$, use cross multiplication to solve for x.

$22 \times 27 = 6x \times 9 \Rightarrow 594 = 54x \Rightarrow x = 11$

39) Answer: A

The probability of choosing a Hearts is $\frac{13}{52} + \frac{13}{52} = \frac{1}{2}$

40) Answer: B

If the score of Harper was 84, therefore the score of Emma is 42. Since, the score of Zoe was one sixth of Emma, therefore, the score of Zoe is 7.

Practice Test 6

STAAR - Mathematics

Answers and Explanations

1) Answer: D

Use Pythagorean Theorem: $a^2 + b^2 = c^2$

$18^2 + 24^2 = C^2 \Rightarrow 324 + 576 = C^2 \Rightarrow 900 = c^2 \Rightarrow \text{c} = 30$

2) Answer: A

Let x be the number. Write the equation and solve for x.

$\frac{(80-x)}{x} = 4$ (cross multiply)

$(80 - x) = 4x$, then add x both sides. $80 = 5x$, now divide both sides by 5. $\Rightarrow x = 16$.

3) Answer: D

Use simple interest formula: $I = prt$;

$(I = interest.p = principal.r = rate.t = time)$

$I = (10{,}000)\ (0.024)\ (3) = 720$

4) Answer: B

Let x be the number of soft drinks for 132 guests. Write the proportion and solve for x.

$\frac{\text{15 soft drinks}}{\text{9 guests}} = \frac{x}{\text{162 guests}} \Rightarrow x = \frac{162 \times 15}{9} \Rightarrow x = 270$

5) Answer: C

16% of the volume of the solution is alcohol. Let x be the volume of the solution. Then:

16% of x = 9.2 ml

$0.16\ x = 9.2 \Rightarrow \frac{16x}{100} = \frac{92}{10}$ cross multiply; $16x = 9{,}200 \Rightarrow$ (devide by 16) $x = 575$

6) Answer: A

Use the area of rectangle formula (S = a × b).

To find area of the shaded region subtract smaller rectangle from bigger rectangle.

$S_1 - S_2 = (7\,ft \times 16ft) - (4ft \times 10ft) \Rightarrow S_1 - S_2 = 72ft.$

7) Answer: D

The weight of 22.3 meters of this rope is: $22.3 \times 210g = 4{,}683g$

1 kg = 1,000 g, therefore, 4,683 $g \div 1000$ = 4.683kg

8) Answer: 130

The ratio of boy to girls is 5:9. Therefore, there are 5 boys out of 14 students. To find the answer, first divide the total number of students by 14, then multiply the result by 5.

$364 \div 14 = 26 \Rightarrow 26 \times 5 = 130$

9) Answer: B

the population is increased by 8% and 14%. 8% increase changes the population to 108% of original population.

For the second increase, multiply the result by 114%.

(1.08) × (1.14) = (1.2312) =123.12 %

23.12 percent of the population is increased after two years.

10)Answer: A

A linear equation is a relationship between two variables, x and y, that can be put in the form $y = mx + b$.

A non-proportional linear relationship takes on the form $y = mx + b$, where $b \neq 0$ and its graph is a line that does not cross through the origin.

11)Answer: B

Four years ago, Amy was three times as old as Mike. Mike is 12 years now. Therefore, 4 years ago Mike was 8 years.

Four years ago, Amy was: $A = 8 \times 3 = 24$

Now Amy is 28 years old: 24 + 4 = 28

12)Answer: A

$|-44 + 15| - |6\,(-3)| = |-29| - |-18| = 29 - 18 = 11$

13)Answer: A

$\begin{cases} \frac{x}{6} + \frac{y}{4} = 2 \\ \frac{-5y}{6} - 2x = -11 \end{cases} \rightarrow$ Multiply the top equation by 12. Then,

$\begin{cases} 2x + 3y = 24 \\ \frac{-5y}{6} - 2x = -11 \end{cases} \rightarrow$ Add two equations.

$\frac{13}{6}y = 13 \rightarrow y = 6$, plug in the value of y into the first equation$\rightarrow x = 3$

14) Answer: C

$\frac{2}{9} \times 45 = \frac{90}{9} = 10$

15) Answer: B

Two triangles ΔABC and ΔCD are similar. Then:

$\frac{\text{AB}}{\text{DF}} = \frac{\text{BC}}{\text{CD}} \rightarrow \frac{3}{4} = \frac{x}{42 - x} \rightarrow 126 - 3x = 4x \rightarrow 7x = 126 \rightarrow x = 18$

16) Answer: D

The slop of line A is: $m = \frac{y_2 - y_1}{x_2 - x_1} = \frac{8-2}{5 - 3} = 3$

Parallel lines have the same slope and only choice D $(4y - 12x = 7 \Rightarrow \text{y} = 3x + \frac{7}{4})$ has slope of 3.

17) Answer: A

The perimeter of the rectangle is: $2x + 2y = 38$

$\rightarrow x + y = 19 \rightarrow x = 19 - y$

The area of the rectangle is: $x \times y = 90 \rightarrow (19 - y)(y) = 90$

$\rightarrow y^2 - 19y + 90 = 0$

Solve the quadratic equation by factoring method.

$(y - 9)(y - 10) = 0 \rightarrow y = 9$ (Unacceptable, because y must be greater than 9) or $y = 10$; If $y = 10 \rightarrow x = 19 - y \rightarrow x = 19 - 10 \rightarrow x = 9$

18) Answer: A

Let x be the number of new shoes the team can purchase. Therefore, the team can purchase 102 x.

The team had \$26,000 and spent \$18,000. Now the team can spend on new shoes \$8,000 at most.

Now, write the inequality: $102x + 18{,}000 \leq 26{,}000$

19) Answer: C

Use the formula for Percent of Change

$\frac{\text{New Value}-\text{Old Value}}{\text{Old Value}} \times 100\ \% \Rightarrow \frac{49-70}{70} \times 100\ \% = -30\ \%$

(negative sign here means that the new price is less than old price).

20) Answer: A

Use simple interest formula: $I = prt$ (I = interest, p = principal, r = rate, t = time)

$I = (11{,}000)(0.025)\ (6) = 1{,}650$

21) Answer: A

Use this formula: Percent of Change = $\frac{\text{New Value}-\text{Old Value}}{\text{Old Value}} \times 100\ \%$

$\frac{42{,}000-56{,}000}{56{,}000} \times 100\ \% = -25\ \%$ and $\frac{31{,}500-42{,}000}{42{,}000} \times 100\% = -25\ \%$

22) Answer: D

The amount of money for x bookshelf is: $86x$

Then, the total cost of all bookshelves is equal to: $86x + 670$

The total cost, in dollar, per bookshelf is: $\frac{Total\ cost}{number\ of\ items} = \frac{86x+670}{x}$

23) Answer: D

A. $f(x) = 2x^2 + 6$ if $x = 8 \rightarrow f(8) = 2(8)^2 + 6 = 134 \neq 14$

B. $f(x) = 4x^2 - 6x + 6$ if $x = 8 \rightarrow f(8) = 4(8)^2 - 6 \times 8 + 6 = 214 \neq 14$

C. $f(x) = \sqrt{2x + 6}$ if $x = 8 \rightarrow f(8) = \sqrt{2(8) + 6} = \sqrt{22} \neq 14$

D. $f(x) = 2\sqrt{2x} + 6$ if $x = 8 \rightarrow f(8) = 2\sqrt{2(8)} + 6 = 14 = 14$

24) Answer: B

Let x be all expenses, then $\frac{22}{100}x = \$880 \rightarrow x = \frac{100 \times \$880}{22} = \$4{,}000$

He spent for his rent: $\frac{34}{100} \times \$4{,}000 = \$1{,}360$

25) Answer: A

The smallest number is -12. To find the largest possible value of one of the other five integers, we need to choose the smallest possible integers for three of them. Let x be the largest number. Then:

$-50 = (-12) + (-11) + (-10) + (-9) + x \rightarrow -50 = -42 + x$

$\rightarrow x = -50 + 42 = -8$

26) Answer: C

The angles on a straight line add up to 180 degrees. Then:

$x + 16 + 2y + 4y + 4x = 180$

Then, $5x + 6y = 180 - 16 \rightarrow 5(10) + 6y = 164 \rightarrow 6y = 164 - 50 = 114 \rightarrow y = 19$

27) Answer: B

Square root of 121 is $\sqrt{121} = 11 > \sqrt{49} = 7$

Square root of 52 is $\sqrt{52} = \sqrt{49 + 3} > \sqrt{49} = 7$

Square root of 81 is $\sqrt{81} = 9 > 7$

Square root of 58 is $\sqrt{58} = \sqrt{49 + 9} > 7$

Since, $\sqrt{52} < \sqrt{58}$, then the answer is B.

28) Answer: C

To find the area of the shaded region subtract smaller circle from bigger circle.

$S_{bigger} - S_{smaller} = \pi (r_{bigger})^2 - \pi (r_{smaller})^2 \Rightarrow S_{bigger} - S_{smaller} = \pi (5)^2 - \pi (3)^2$

$\Rightarrow 25\pi - 9\pi = 16\pi$

29) Answer: D

$\sqrt{x} = -5 \rightarrow x = 25$

then; $\sqrt{x} - 4 = \sqrt{25} - 4 = 5 - 4 = 1$ and $\sqrt{3x + 6} = \sqrt{75 + 6} = \sqrt{81} = 9$Then:

$\left(\sqrt{3x + 6}\right) + \left(\sqrt{x} - 4\right) = 9 + 1 = 10$

30) Answer: 98.

$a = 14 \Rightarrow$ area of the triangle is

$= \frac{1}{2}(14 \times 14) = \frac{196}{2} = 98\ cm^2$

Isosceles right triangle

a

a

31) Answer: A

x is directly proportional to the square of y. Then: $x = cy^2$

$63 = c(3)^2 \rightarrow 63 = 9c \rightarrow c = \frac{63}{9} = 7$

The relationship between x and y is: $x = 7y^2$, $x = 175$

$175 = 7y^2 \rightarrow y^2 = \frac{175}{7} = 25 \rightarrow y = 5$

32) Answer: C

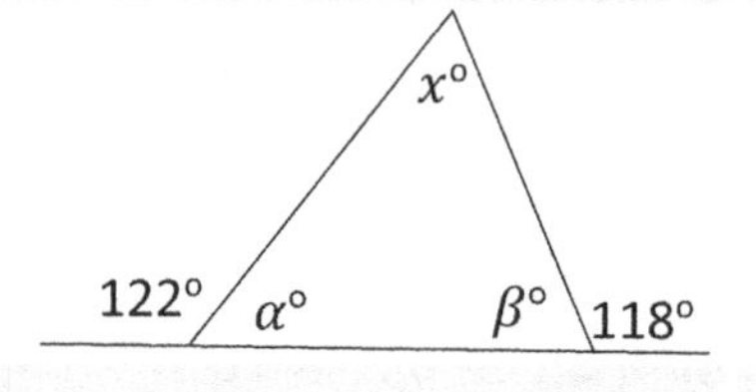

$\alpha = 180^{\circ} - 122^{\circ} = 58^{\circ}$

$\beta = 180^{\circ} - 118^{\circ} = 62^{\circ}$

$x + \alpha + \beta = 180^{\circ} \rightarrow x = 180^{\circ} - 58^{\circ} - 62^{\circ} = 60^{\circ}$

33) Answer: 3

Use formula of rectangle prism volume.

V = (length) (width) (height) ⇒ 1,344 = (32) (14) (height) ⇒ height = 1,344 ÷ 448 = 3

34) Answer: C

The amount of money that jack earns for one hour: $\frac{\$500}{25} = \$20$

Number of additional hours that he works to make enough money is: $\frac{\$920-\$500}{1.5\times\$20} = 14$

Number of total hours is: $20 + 14 = 34$

35) Answer: C

Let's find the mean (average), mode and median of the number of cities for each type of pollution.

Number of cities for each type of pollution: 6, 3, 2, 9, 4

average (mean) = $\frac{sum\ of\ terms}{number\ of\ terms} = \frac{6+3+2+9+4}{5} = \frac{24}{5} = 4.8$

Median is the number in the middle. To find median, first list numbers in order from smallest to largest: 2, 3, 4, 6, 9

Median of the data is 4.

Mode is the number which appears most often in a set of numbers. Therefore, there is no mode in the set of numbers.

Median < Mean, then, $c < a$

36) Answer: B

Let the number of cities should be added to type of pollutions B be x. Then:

$\frac{x+3}{9} = 1 \rightarrow x + 3 = 9 \times 1 \rightarrow x + 3 = 9 \rightarrow x = 6$

37) Answer: A

Percent of cities in the type of pollution A: $\frac{6}{10} \times 100 = 60\%$

Percent of cities in the type of pollution C: $\frac{2}{10} \times 100 = 20\%$

Percent of cities in the type of pollution E: $\frac{4}{10} \times 100 = 40\%$

38) Answer: C

$AB = 6$, And $AC = 8$

$BC = \sqrt{6^2 + 8^2} = \sqrt{36 + 64} = \sqrt{100} = 10$

Perimeter $= 6 + 8 + 10 = 24$; Area $= \frac{6 \times 8}{2} = 24$

In this case, the ratio of the perimeter of the triangle to its area is: $\frac{24}{24} = 1$

If the sides AB and AC become half longer, then: $AB = 3$, And $AC = 4$

$BC = \sqrt{3^2 + 4^2} = \sqrt{9 + 16} = \sqrt{25} = 5$

Perimeter $= 3 + 4 + 5 = 12$; Area $= \frac{3 \times 4}{2} = 3 \times 2 = 6$

In this case the ratio of the perimeter of the triangle to its area is: $\frac{12}{6} = 2$

39) Answer: C

The capacity of a red box is 30% bigger than the capacity of a blue box and it can hold 78 books. Therefore, we want to find a number that 30% bigger than that number is 78. Let x be that number. Then:

$1.30 \times x = 78$, Divide both sides of the equation by 1.3. Then: $x = \frac{78}{1.30} = 60$

40) Answer: D

$\$15 \times 6 = \$90$

Petrol use: $3 \div 2 = 1.5$. $6 \times 1.5 = 9$ liters

Petrol cost: $9 \times \$2.2 = \$19.8$

Money earned: $\$90 - \$19.8 = \$70.2$

"End"

Made in the USA
Coppell, TX
23 June 2022

79166662R00079